Endorsements for
Truth Tellers: The Power and Presence of Black Women Journalists Since 1960

"The first Black woman to run for vice president of the United States was Charlotta Bass - a journalist. That happened 70 years ago.

For nearly four decades before her 1952 run for the vice presidency, Bass was the crusading editor and publisher of the California Eagle, the largest Black-owned newspaper on the West Coast. But those who write the history of that time have largely forgotten—or simply ignored—Bass.

Bonnie Newman Davis' book, *Truth Tellers: The Power and Presence of Black Women Journalists Since 1960*, tells the stories of 24 Black women whose journalism careers spanned the last forty years of the 20th century. They are print and broadcast journalists and, like Bass, courageously bore the burden of being a Black person in America's newsrooms.

Norma Adams-Wade to Lynne K. Varner, Wanda Lloyd to Barbara Ciara, and Patrice Gaines to Sandra Daye Hughes, the stories Davis tells are of Black women journalists who took on the challenges of being what W.E.B. DuBois called the "two-ness" of being an American and Black.

These women aren't household names. This book, hopefully, will change that."

DeWayne Wickham
Journalist, Columnist and Founding Dean
School of Global Journalism & Communication
Morgan State University

"America replaced its race-based slavery with a system of full racial apartheid, which lasted 100-plus years. What we would today term the mainstream media was a full partner in our American apartheid. Plus, journalism was essentially a man's world and hardly an easy ecosystem for Black women to enter, let alone in which to excel. All 24 women journalists profiled in Truth Tellers: The Power and Presence of Black Women Journalists Since 1960 have compelling stories, exquisitely presented by Bonnie Newman Davis. This book is much needed and is required reading for us all."

John R. Rich, Philanthropist
Greensboro, North Carolina

"Anthologies on Black women journalists tend to focus on pioneers who broke new ground during the 19th century or broke barriers as correspondents during the first half of the 20th century. Truth Tellers: The Power and Presence of Black Women Journalists Since 1960 shares the stories of 24 Black women journalists. It explores the challenges they faced in entering and existing in contemporary white newsrooms after the civil rights movement and the 1968 Kerner Commission Report, which criticized newspapers and television for their inadequate and sometimes demeaning coverage of Black communities and failure to diversify their newsrooms.

These 24 women share what inspired them to become journalists and why telling the stories of Black people and their communities was so important. Through their steadfast commitment to the pursuit of truth through the practice of excellent journalism, and most of all, by their mere presence, they have had a significant impact on the next generation of not just Black women journalists but journalists, storytellers, and strategic communicators as a whole.

This long overdue and much-needed collection is a perfect companion to more recent memoirs from Black women journalists like Carole Simpson, Belva Davis, and Dorothy Butler Gilliam."

Trevy McDonald, Ph.D., Associate Professor of Journalism
The University of North Carolina at Chapel Hill

"While we have become accustomed to seeing Black women journalists on screen, there are so many who are lesser known and unsung, but who have paved important paths in the field. Bonnie Newman Davis lifts their names and tells their important stories. This is an important book for students and scholars who want (need) to know the full history of journalism."

Tamara Jeffries, Journalist,
Former Executive Editor, Essence Magazine

"There is so much power in the pages of this book. As Black journalists, this is the lost handbook of who we have been and who we will push forward to be. I only wish I could have had this when I started. Legacy is everything."

Andrea King Collier, Award-winning Journalist and Columnist

"*Truth Tellers: The Power and Presence of Black Women Journalists Since 1960* introduces readers to "two dozen women whose names may or may not be familiar," author Bonnie Newman Davis says. After reading their stories, you'll realize that all of these skilled, remarkable women should be as recognizable as any other journalist of the era. I'm proud to know some of these journalists as my friends and former colleagues, and I'm grateful to Bonnie Davis for bringing their stories to the world—especially to young women journalists of color who will find inspiration and determination in every chapter."

Jane Elizabeth, Journalist

"When I think of Bonnie Newman Davis' book, *Truth Tellers: The Power and Presence of Black Women Journalists Since 1960*, I think of two words: hidden figures. Brilliant, bold and beautiful Black women are often unseen and unheard due to racism and misogyny. Davis teaches us about Black women who are pioneers in a reputable, powerful and transformative profession—journalism. We know the power that journalists wield. What many of us did not know is the crucial roles that Black women journalists have played over the years. As a well-known Black actress said during an awards ceremony several years ago, "Hidden figures no more."

Linnie Smith Carter, Ph.D., Vice President of College Advancement at HACC, Central Pennsylvania's Community College

"Twenty-four Black women featured here include a daily newspaper publisher, White House correspondent, and longtime mid-market TV anchor and managing editor. Many of the rest were local news reporters who consciously committed to cover their communities. What all of these women have in common is their significance as civil rights-era or late 20th century trailblazers who profoundly changed the American news media from within. Bravo."

Wayne Dawkins, *Author of*
The NABJ Story and Rugged Waters: Black Journalists

"Bonnie Newman Davis has curated this collection of stories about Black women journalists in four movements with a reporter's eye, an editor's perspective and a historian's sensitivity to research. The career of each barrier-breaking, trailblazing news leader teaches indispensable lessons about navigating the media field while meeting the challenges of life in America."

Linda Shockley, Former Managing Director,
Dow Jones News Fund

"Bonnie Newman Davis's journalistic achievements run the gamut. However, she recognizes her success could not have been possible without the African American female journalists who paved the way—not only before her, but also, alongside her. In the book, Truth Tellers: The Power and Presence of Black Women Journalists Since 1960, she presents the powerful stories of 24 journalists who succeeded despite the incredible odds against them. Some of them experienced humiliation and depression; others faced backlash from within their own communities. Yet, their dedication to truth and purpose prevailed, providing a much-needed inspirational blueprint for a new generation of journalists navigating tumultuous times."

Karla Redditte, Anchor, Spectrum News 1

"It is often said today that women are the face of journalism, with demographics shifting and placing them in the majority in our classrooms and newsrooms. Bonnie Newman Davis offers us a very special invitation to consider that perhaps they always have been. This timely and much needed assessment of the journeys and achievements of Black women of our time fills a void that long has existed in telling the story of the journalism profession. I'm proud and pleased to say I know many of these women and have seen them in action firsthand. They have been and continue to be difference makers. Those I did not know before now, I get to know because Bonnie has sagaciously pulled together chapters of their lives and placed them within reach. The bonus is, in telling their stories, Bonnie is also telling her own amazing story, which needs to be known and shared with all aspiring journalists, regardless of gender or color. Write on Sister Bonnie."

Robbie R. Morganfield, Ph.D., Chair, Department of Journalism and Mass Communication, North Carolina A&T State University

TRUTH TELLERS

The Power and Presence of Black Women Journalists Since 1960

TRUTH TELLERS

The Power and Presence of Black Women Journalists Since 1960

BONNIE NEWMAN DAVIS

Copyright © 2022 by Bonnie Newman Davis.
All rights reserved.

No part of this book may be reproduced, stored in a retrieval system or transmitted in any form or by any means without the prior written permission of the publisher—except by a reviewer who may quote brief passages in a review to be printed in a newspaper, magazine or journal. For inquiry contact the publisher.

Although this publication is designed to provide accurate information in regard to the subject matter covered, the publisher and the author assume no responsibility for errors, inaccuracies, omissions, or any other inconsistencies herein.

Published by:
BND Institute of Media & Culture
(276) 254-8742

ISBN: 978-0-578-29935-8

Library of Congress Control Number: 2022917481

Book Cover Design: Visual Appeal, LLC

Interior Design: TWA Solutions.com

Printed in the United States of America

For my beloved daughter, Erin Danielle Stanley; for my late husband, William H. Davis, who was the wind beneath my wings; and for my parents, James Allen Newman, Sr. and Dorothy Chavis Newman, whose enduring love and spirit continue to guide me.

"The words were living things to her. She sensed them bestriding the air and charging the room with strong colors."

—Paule Marshall, *Brown Girl, Brownstone*

"A loud voice is not always angry; a soft voice not always to be dismissed; and a well-placed silence can be the indisputable last word."

—Gloria Naylor, "Finding Our Voice: 11 Black Women Writers Speak," *Essence*

Contents

Preface xvii
Introduction xxi

Part 1: Maynard Institute and NABJ

Chapter 1: *Denise Bridges:* A Career Framed by Police Brutality—Navigating Newsrooms, Racial Strife, and Political Minefields 1

Chapter 2: *Fannie Flono:* Curiosity and Persistence Propel Her Career—Words as Weapons for Slaying 9

Chapter 3: *Norma Adams-Wade:* Just the Facts, Please—Recording Momentous Hometown History for Fifty Years ... 17

Chapter 4: *Dorothy Butler Gilliam*: A Legendary Trailblazer and Pioneer—From Alienation to Spiritual Leadership 26

Chatper 5: *Robin Farmer:* A Witness to the Truth—A Clear-Eyed Childhood Scripted Her Future 32

Part 2: From Setbacks to Success

Chapter 6: *Lynne K. Varner:* Unheeding the Headwinds—Crafting a Career with Intention and Purpose 39

Chatper 7: *Sheila Robinson Solomon:* When Patience Becomes the Best Equalizer—Providing Relief and Solace Becomes Her Legacy 48

Chapter 8: *Wanda Lloyd:* Pushing Back, Moving Forward—
Education and Tenacity Led to Journalism's Pinnacle 57

Chapter 9: *Patrice Gaines:* Laughing in the Dark—In
Advocating for the "Underdog," She
Advocates for Everyone 69

Chapter 10: *Barbara Ciara:* "Fall Down, Get Up, Don't
Whine"—From Early Missteps to Broadcast Stardom 78

Chapter 11: *Sandra C. Dillard:* Bright Lights, Big Cities
Fuel Passion for Journalism—From the Classroom to
World Stages, Creativity Played a Leading Role 86

Part 3: Changing How Communities Are Covered

Chapter 12. *Cassandra Spratling:* Chronicling the Events and
Sacrifices of Everyday People—Detroit Is Center Stage for
Covering the Extraordinary and Ordinary for Forty Years 97

Chapter 13: *Mae Israel:* Speaking, with Authority and
Passion, for Black Lives—Overcoming Speech Impediment,
Racism, and Sexism to Find Career Success 103

Chapter 14: *Felecia Henderson:* A Voice for the Community—
A Defining Moment Inspires Renewed Purpose 111

Chapter 15: *Diane Graham Walker:* Reporting Truth to Realize
Power—Dedicated Consumer Advocate Reaps Results 118

Chapter 16: *Sonya Ross:* Cultivating Sources Others Ignored—
From Covering the White House to Becoming Unmuted ... 127

Chapter 17: *Teresa J. Styles:* Blending Black Voices into the "Way It Was" at *CBS News*—Broadcast Pioneer's Pivotal Lessons for Students.. 136

Part 4: Racing to the Top

Chapter 18: *Pamela McAllister Johnson:* Ambition, Confidence, and a Rapid Ascent—Opportunity Knocked, Enabling Her to Be Called "First".. 147

Chapter 19: *Deborah Heard:* Quiet Power in the Newsroom—Self-Possessed Manner Guided Her Path to Management... 155

Chapter 20: *Sandra Daye Hughes:* Daring to Be Seen, Heard, and Respected—Building a Lasting, Illustrious Career at Her Hometown News Station 161

Chapter 21: *Lynn Norment: Ebony* Exclusives: From Al Green to Tina Turner—Determination, Grit Gave Her Rarefied Access to Black Celebrities 167

Chapter 22: *Stacy Hawkins Adams:* Charting a Path with Words That Resonate—Journalism Propelled Book Career and a Desire to Uplift Others 175

Chapter 23: *Angela P. Dodson:* A Window on Life and Death—Steely Reserve for Covering Unspeakable Disasters in Places High and Low.. 181

Chapter 24: *Yanick Rice Lamb:* Considering All Things and More—Empathy for the Voiceless Guides Her Purpose....... 190

Epilogue 197
Index... 201

Preface

I left daily journalism in 1999 to teach and navigate online journalism at a time when most newspapers had yet to fully embrace new media and technology. Academia's "publish or perish" mantra was incessant, but meant little to me, a print journalist who had been writing professionally since my first internship at the *Wilmington (NC) Star News* in 1978. When academic colleagues suggested that writing a book was preferable to writing about topics that drive daily news gathering, I instinctively knew to write about Black women journalists who also entered the nation's newsrooms after the often turbulent civil rights movement of the 1960s.

Although Black women had worked in newsrooms prior to and during the civil rights era, dozens more entered the industry following the *1968 Kerner Commission Report*, a National Advisory Commission on Civil Disorders, that concluded the nation was moving toward two societies—one Black, one white. Legislation encouraging a more equitable society was urged, and the news media, blamed for ignoring or sublimating much of the societal unrest, was pressured to employ more Blacks.

I was 11 years old when the report was released and, although I was by then enrolled in a racially integrated school, I knew little about civil rights with the exception of Reverend Dr. Martin Luther King, Jr.'s assassination that same year. I had previously lived within walking distance of Greensboro's Woolworth's department store where, eight years earlier, North Carolina A&T State University students' nonviolent stance for equal rights had mobilized a nation.

Another five years would pass before I would see the results of Kerner and other quests for equal opportunity when an African American woman suddenly was seen dispensing the news in my hometown of Greensboro, North Carolina. Her name was Sandra Daye Hughes and I recall her visiting Walter Hines Page High School when I became a student there. A connection was made with Hughes's appearance: She had majored in English as a student at A&T, but could not find a teaching job after graduating. Hughes then one day walked into WFMY-TV station on Phillips Avenue, a short distance from my home in Greensboro's Woodmere Park neighborhood, and was hired.

Years later, long after I had entered A&T myself, majored in English, wrote for the school newspaper, dabbled in television and radio under the tutelage of professors such as Loreno Marrow, Richard E. Moore, Ronald Topping, Gregory Lewis, and Phillip Jeter, I often thought about Sandra Hughes and other Black women journalists who had carved careers in newsrooms throughout the country. Ultimately, I would follow their paths into newsrooms in Wilmington, North Carolina; Louisville, Kentucky; Ann Arbor, Michigan; and Richmond, Virginia.

When I became a contributing writer and later editor of the NABJ Journal (from 2006 to 2014), I often interviewed and wrote about prominent Black male journalists such as William Raspberry, Lerone Bennett, and Dean Baquet. Rarely, it seemed, did the magazine's articles focus on Black women journalists, despite the significant role of women such as Ida B. Wells, Alice Allison Dunnigan, and Ethel Payne during the 1930s, 1940s, and 1950s, and despite the fact that several women had served as NABJ's president since its creation in 1975. Certainly, the contributions of post–civil rights era journalists such as Charlayne Hunter-Gault, Dorothy Butler Gilliam (a former NABJ president), Gwen Ifill, and Sandra Hughes are not only admired, but equally significant.

In this book—truly a labor of love—you will meet two dozen women whose names may or may not be familiar. Their stories are engaging, endearing and like any good book, full of surprises. Indeed, in writing this book, I found myself amazed, angry, laughing, or weeping. Most of all, I discovered a deep, abiding connection with these women whose stories reflect my own—whether in our thirst for education and knowledge,

Preface

appreciation for words and language, a determination to enter and succeed in unknown spaces, and an incessant desire to help others find their voice and tell their stories.

It is my hope that after reading about these women, you also will be as inspired and appreciative for the determination and sacrifice made in numerous ways by these journalists whose commitment to the cause enable many of them to still tell our stories in ways that make us think, grow and learn.

I am forever indebted to and grateful for John R. Rich, who challenged me to write this book and provided emotional and financial support during the seven years that it took to complete this work. Andre Barnett is owed a special "thank you" for her expert editing, unending patience, and gentle touch during this lengthy process. I also appreciate the support of Janet Davenport, my longtime NABJ colleague who not only introduced me to Andre, but said "yes" when I begged her to be my "accountability" coach. Without Janet's soothing, yet firm coaching and feedback, this book would exist only as hard-to-read handwritten notes on yellow legal pads.

Cathy Gant Hill, Michelle Fitzhugh-Craig, Tammie Smith, Sadeqa Johnson, Harriet McLeod, Cathy M. Jackson, Janet Davenport (again), Laurie Willis, Robin Adams, Marjorie Vaughn, Debora Timms and Neldera Weathersbee graciously agreed to author, edit or critique several chapters in this book. Sterling advice from Dr. Trevy McDonald, Wayne Dawkins, DeWayne Wickham, Yolanda McCutchen, Karla Peters, Sabrina Squire, Dr. Linnie S. Carter, Otesa Middleton Miles, Jane Isay, Ann Jeffries, Jessica Tilles, Nickkol Lewis, Lydia Thompson, Craig Cotton, and Christine Hoskin always came at the right moment. I overflow with joy for the total support from my aunt, Winfry Jean Chavis Grube, and from dear friends Deborah Walker Burns, Sarah Brown James, Dawn Cunningham, Lee Ivory, Angela McCrae, Chinae Massenberg, Vinara Mosby, Renee Walston Johnson, L. Michael Harvey, Teshana Gipson-Stinson, Cyril and Vanessa Coombs, Patrick L. Riley, Trudy Moore, Vanessa G. Cunningham, Linda Conway, Shirley McMullen,

Truth Tellers: *The Power and Presence of Black Women Journalists Since 1960*

Betty Thompson Morton, Kym Grinnage and Wheeler Brown. A special thank you to Sarah Glover, Dorothy Tucker, Angela Robinson and the National Association of Black Journalists for supporting this book with an Inaugural Creators' Grant, a gesture that further attests to how crucial the organization has been in my career and journey since I attended my first NABJ convention in 1980.

Also, thank you to everyone who has ever believed in me, especially my daughter, Erin Danielle Stanley; my parents, the late James A. Newman, Sr. and the late Dorothy Chavis Newman; my four siblings, James, Christopher Noelle, Sally, and Dickie; and my late husband, William Haynes Davis.

Above all, "thank you" to the twenty-four brave women who agreed to share—through countless interviews and conversations—intimate details of their professional and personal lives. Their willingness to be a part of this work reflects an abiding belief that this is an important text to be treasured by future generations of African American women journalists. Ida B. Wells, perhaps the most prominent Black woman journalist, said it best: "*The people must know before they can act, and there is no educator to compare with the press.*"

Introduction

Norma Adams-Wade was a sophomore at the University of Texas when she learned that President John F. Kennedy, a popular president held in high regard by Black Americans, had been assassinated in her hometown of Dallas at age 46. The shocking news came just months after Alabama Governor George C. Wallace physically blocked two Black students from registering at the University of Alabama in Tuscaloosa. Wallace, a staunch segregationist, did not back down until President Kennedy sent the National Guard to the campus. Another racially charged event that year included the August 29 March on Washington for Jobs and Freedom, which drew 250,000 people to hear the Reverend Dr. Martin Luther King, Jr., deliver his "I Have A Dream" speech in front of the Lincoln Memorial. Less than a month after King's speech, on September 15, 1963, a bomb at the 16th Street Baptist Church in Birmingham, Alabama, killed four young girls and injured several other people prior to Sunday services.

On August 11, 1965, Marquette Frye, a young African American motorist, was pulled over and arrested by Lee W. Minikus, a white California highway patrol officer, for suspicion of driving while intoxicated near Los Angeles, California. When onlookers gathered at the scene of Frye's arrest, a violent exchange erupted between the crowd and police.

The outbreak led to a six-day riot in the commercial section of Watts, a deeply impoverished African American neighborhood in South Central

Los Angeles. By the time order was restored on August 17, 34 people were dead, more than 1,000 had been injured, and nearly 4,000 arrested.

Watching the televised riots, filled with fighting, looting, burning automobiles, and thousands of National Guard troops, was 14-year-old Denise Bridges, née Robertson. While gripped by the scenes flashing before her, something else caught Bridges' attention.

"Look! Come look! There's a Black man doing the news," Bridges' mother screamed to anyone within earshot.

Seeing a Black man deliver the news during a time when riots and social unrest rocked cities throughout the United States not only heightened Bridges' interest in journalism but most likely propelled it. Back then, Black people seldom were seen on television in anything but subservient, stereotypical, or comedic roles or in sports.

In 1961, 23-year-old Dorothy Butler Gilliam, armed with a master's degree in journalism from Columbia University, stepped into the *Washington Post*'s newsroom to become the first Black woman, and the second African American, to be hired as a reporter at the venerable newspaper. Gilliam, an award-winning journalist who sharpened her reporting and writing skills in high school and then college working for the *Black Press*, blazed trails in and out of the newsroom. She paid dearly for her pioneering efforts, which included feeling isolated, humiliated, and even experiencing anxiety and depression as she battled to build her venerable career.

Many of her white colleagues, including other women also breaking new professional ground, alienated her. Taxicabs would not stop for her. When she showed up for assignments, white and Black Washingtonians questioned her press credentials. In retrospect, Gilliam said her initial professional expectations were "naive" as she went on to break color and gender barriers.

Introduction

Civil rights luminary Rosa Parks moved to Detroit in 1957, two years after igniting the Montgomery Bus Boycott on December 1, 1955. That is the same date that Cassandra Spratling, who would later interview Parks for the *Detroit Free Press*, was born.

To celebrate the fortieth anniversary of the Montgomery Bus Boycott in 1995, *Detroit Free Press* journalist Cassandra Spratling interviewed domestic workers who walked to their jobs during the 381-day boycott rather than ride the segregated buses of Montgomery. In a rare moment, Spratling cried as one woman explained her nightly ritual for more than a year: Epsom-salt footbaths to ease her pain.

Spratling's decision to write about the not-so-famous protesters instead of the iconic Rosa Parks, who, in the years following her historic 1955 bus boycott for civil rights, moved from Alabama to Detroit, was intentional. As much as she adored Parks, she knew that the courage and strength displayed by hundreds of others seeking change was equally important.

"I will never forget being in that woman's living room," Spratling said. "She still had the basin where she would soak her feet. I said, 'How did you do that'? I felt like I wanted to kiss her feet. She did this for me. I wouldn't have been there interviewing her had she not done that."

Memories of the 1960s remain swollen with news of racial injustice and discrimination aimed at Black people in America.

The Woolworth's Lunch Counter protests in 1960, the Civil Rights Act of 1964, the Voting Rights Act of 1965, the Fair Housing Act of 1968 and Motown all were instrumental in strengthening our confidence, lifting our spirits and giving us hope for a brighter future. Early in the decade, much of that progress would have been minimized without televised news media coverage showing fire hoses and vicious dogs unleashed on civil rights protesters in the South. Such actions prompted Americans to pay closer attentions to the horrible treatment of Blacks who were simply seeking a better way of life for themselves and their children. Yet, as the decade neared an end, the deaths of Malcolm X, the Reverend Dr. Martin Luther King, Jr., and Robert F. Kennedy (the brother of President John F. Kennedy who was slain in 1963), and other civil rights activists sparked further and often violent unrest that continued to pierce the nation, particularly during the summer of 1967 when a bar raid in Detroit triggered a five-day war between the city's Black residents and the Detroit Police Department. By the end of the bloody battle, 43 people were dead, 1,189 were injured and more than 7,200 were arrested. After Detroit, dozens of riots repeatedly erupted throughout the country, prompting President Lyndon B. Johnson to establish the National Advisory Commission on Civil Disorders, commonly known as the Kerner Commission Report, to investigate the causes of the riots and make recommendations for the future.

The report, released in early 1968 after a seven-month investigation, blamed the riots on the lack of economic opportunity among Blacks, failed social service programs, police brutality, racism, and the white-oriented media. It concluded that the nation was "moving toward two societies, one Black, one white—separate and unequal." Unless conditions were remedied, the Commission warned, the country faced a "system of 'apartheid'" in its major cities. The Kerner report also delivered an indictment of "white society" for isolating and neglecting African Americans and urged legislation to promote racial integration and to enrich slums—primarily through the creation of jobs, job training programs, and decent housing. President Johnson, however, rejected the recommendations. In April 1968, one month after the release of the Kerner report, rioting broke out in more than one hundred cities following the assassination of civil rights leader Martin Luther King, Jr. Although the report noted that the majority of news media accounts did not sensationalize their coverage, the Kerner Commission agreed that the nation's newspapers and magazines failed to adequately report on African American life:

News organizations must employ enough Negroes in positions of significant responsibility to establish an effective link to Negro actions and ideas and

Introduction

to meet legitimate employment expectations. Tokenism—the hiring of one Negro reporter, or even two or three—is no longer enough. Negro reporters are essential, but so are Negro editors, writers and commentators. Newspaper and television policies are, generally speaking, not set by reporters. Editorial decisions about which stories to cover and which to use are made by editors. Yet, very few Negroes in this country are involved in making these decisions, because very few, if any, supervisory editorial jobs are held by Negroes. We urge the news media to do everything possible to train and promote their Negro reporters to positions where those who are qualified can contribute to and have an effect on policy decisions (http://historymatters.gmu.edu/d/6553/).

Today, fifty-four years after the Kerner report, memories of the turbulent 1960s are intertwined with news of continuing racial injustice and discrimination aimed at Black people in America.

PART 1

Maynard Institute and NABJ

Chapter 1

Denise Bridges

A Career Framed by Police Brutality—Navigating Newsrooms, Racial Strife, and Political Minefields

Marquette Frye, a young African American motorist, was pulled over and arrested by Lee W. Minikus, a white California highway patrol officer, for suspicion of driving while intoxicated. This was August 11, 1965, near Los Angeles, California. When onlookers gathered at the scene of Frye's arrest, a violent exchange erupted between the crowd and police.

The outbreak led to a six-day riot in the commercial section of Watts, a deeply impoverished African American neighborhood in South Central Los Angeles. By the time order was restored on August 17, 34 people were dead, more than 1,000 had been injured, and nearly 4,000 arrested.

Watching the televised riots filled with fighting, looting, burning automobiles, and thousands of National Guard troops, was 14-year-old Denise Robertson. While gripped by the scenes flashing before her, something else caught Robertson's attention.

"Look! Come look! There's a Black man doing the news," her mother screamed to anyone within earshot.

Seeing a Black man deliver the news during a time when riots and social unrest rocked cities throughout the United States not only heightened Robertson's interest in journalism but most likely propelled it. Back then, Black people seldom were seen on television in anything but subservient, stereotypical, comedic roles or sports.

Fifty years later, Robertson, now Denise Bridges, recalls news being an important element in her Los Angeles home when she was growing up. Her mother was a voracious reader, and *Ebony*, the *Saturday Evening Post*, and the *Los Angeles Times* were household staples.

"There was always information coming into the house. I knew that journalism was something I wanted to do."

Yet, until seeing someone of her race on television delivering the news, Bridges' only journalism role models were the comic book characters Lois Lane and Brenda Starr.

"When I was coming up in the 1950s and 1960s, women didn't have a 'career,' so my admiration was based around these mythical figures. Of course, I later found that it wasn't all that glamorous. But at that point, my mother made sure I paid attention to the news."

Fast forward ten years and two children later, when Bridges enrolled in Los Angeles City College. One of her instructors, Joseph Dojcsak, encouraged her to consider writing for the college newspaper.

Dojcsak "saw something in me that I didn't see in myself," Bridges said. "So, I joined the college newspaper, *The Collegian*, which came out daily or at least three or four times a week. Mr. Dojcsak helped me focus on reporting. I did news, features, and other kinds of stories."

Bridges pauses, motioning toward a stack of books on her kitchen table in Williamsburg, Virginia, her home since 1999. The books contain yellowed clippings from her early reporting years.

"I loved seeing my byline, but even more, I loved meeting people. It would get me into their lives."

With Dojcsak's help, Bridges eventually transferred to the University of Southern California, a private institution that provided scholarships. She spent two years working for the acclaimed student newspaper, the *Daily Trojan*, as a reporter and editor. Armed with a 4.0 grade point average, the Phi Beta Kappa member graduated from USC in 1977.

In 1976, the summer before graduation, Bridges headed to Wilmington, Delaware, her birthplace, for a planned summer internship at the *News-Journal*. She arranged the internship mostly by mail, submitting clips of stories she had accumulated. But when she showed up on the first day, the human resources director looked surprised to see her and told her no job was waiting for her.

"He said there had been a mistake, that the internship was no longer available, but I could have a summer job as an editorial assistant in the sports department. I took it." An editor assigned Bridges to write movie reviews, so she was able to build a portfolio of new clips.

As Bridges and dozens, perhaps hundreds, of other African Americans ascended to newsrooms throughout the country, they were being watched by a handful of prominent African American journalists similar to the Black reporter Bridges saw "doing the news" a dozen years earlier.

These men and women were among pioneering minority journalists recruited by majority white newsrooms during the turbulent 1960s. Their hiring was encouraged after the infamous Kerner Commission Report was initiated by President Lyndon B. Johnson to identify the source of the nation's violent 1967 riots. A key finding in the Kerner Report noted the lack of African Americans working in the nation's mainstream newsroom.

A few years after the release of the Kerner Commission report, Bob and Nancy Maynard marched into Bridges' life. The Maynards were part of a team of journalists who helped found the Summer Program for Minority Journalists, first at Columbia University and later moved to the University of California at Berkeley, an initiative intended to "remove from the American lexicon and the newspaper industry the phrase 'we couldn't find anyone qualified.'" In order to give full support to the program, Maynard left his job at the *Washington Post*, where he had been the first full-time African American reporter. His wife, Nancy, had reported for the *New York Times*. The Maynards later purchased the *Oakland Tribune* from Gannett and championed newsroom diversity like no other news organization. In addition to its award-winning editorials and community coverage, the *Tribune* also won the Pulitzer Prize in 1990 for its compelling photo coverage of the 1989 Loma Prieta earthquake.

The Summer Program for Minority Journalists, which Bridges attended in 1977, trained several hundred journalists and later morphed into the Institute for Journalism Education, expanding its training programs into editing and management. The key feature of many of these programs was job placement.

Following Maynard's death in 1993, IJE was renamed the Maynard Institute for Journalism Education and continues to lead the nationwide effort to diversify American news organizations through its consulting and training programs.

After graduating from the twelve-week program, Bridges was hired at the Associated Press in Los Angeles from 1977 to 1979.

"At AP, I did a little bit of everything; there was only one other Black person out of thirty-three people and one Asian American in the bureau. I would get confused with the other Black woman all the time, even though we didn't look anything alike. We took to calling ourselves 'interchangeable parts.' But it was a good job and I thought I could stay there.

"But two years into AP, Bob Maynard was named editor of the *Oakland Tribune*. When I called to congratulate him, he wanted to know why my resume wasn't on his desk. Two weeks later I was hired as an education writer working under a Black editor. It was wonderful working there. I later covered business and general assignment. After six years Bob wanted me to apply for a Nieman Fellowship, but I got a call from the California Teachers Association to join its communications staff. I thought that sounded exciting. Bob was crushed. I took the job and it lasted eighteen months."

Layoffs at the teachers' association left Bridges without work for months. With her home nearing foreclosure, she was ready to accept a job as a forklift operator. Her luck turned just in time when the Maynard Institute again entered her life. Then president Steve Montiel called and offered her a job as program director. This time, she was the one helping place journalists of color in jobs around the country.

Denise Bridges at The Associated Press in 1979.

"That was in 1989. I stayed there for three years, traveling and recruiting people for the management training program. I left after three years because I went through a divorce and wanted a change, so I decided to attend graduate school to get an MBA. I took a short trip to Albuquerque to visit a friend and clear my head, and decided to apply to business school at the University of New Mexico. While there, I worked for the *Albuquerque Tribune* as a part-time copy editor. Once out of grad school, I wasn't sure what I wanted to do. That's when Gannett talked me into going to the *Tennessean* as a team editor." She was offered the job the same day she interviewed and accepted on the spot.

Bridges soon regretted her decision. Gannett, the *Tennessean*'s parent company, awarded "points" to newspaper leadership through its management by objective program. While senior leaders gained points—and financial bonuses—for meeting various objectives, including minority hiring, they exhibited a laissez-faire attitude toward Bridges: she had no designated workspace and received little support in establishing a relationship with her team.

"That was a painful lesson," she said. "Don't take a job without sleeping on it or connecting with someone else. I felt I wasn't doing a good job, so I asked to move to the copy desk. I also got sick with double pneumonia, for which I was hospitalized for ten days, and then was out of work for six weeks after a hysterectomy. I felt it was not a good place for me. Plus, I was the only minority manager."

As with America's racially charged riots of the 1960s, issues of race and class often defined the 1990s. In March 1991, construction worker Rodney Glen King was violently beaten by Los Angeles Police Department officers for fleeing and resisting arrest on California State Route 210. The beating was recorded by a civilian and sent to a local news station. Four officers were tried on charges of using police brutality; three were acquitted, and the jury failed to reach a verdict on one charge for the fourth. Within hours of the acquittals, the 1992 Los Angeles riots started, sparked by outrage among African Americans over the trial's verdict and related, long-standing social issues. The rioting lasted six days and killed 63 people with 2,383 more injured; it ended only after the California Army National Guard, the United States Army, and the United States Marine Corps provided reinforcements to re-establish control. In separate civil rights cases, two officers were found guilty, and the other two were acquitted.

In 1994, acclaimed athlete and actor O. J. Simpson was arrested and charged with the murders of his ex-wife, Nicole Brown Simpson, and her friend, Ron Goldman. Nicole Simpson and Goldman were white. Simpson was acquitted by a jury after a lengthy and internationally publicized trial.

A year later, in 1995, Nation of Islam Minister Louis Farrakhan called for the Million Man March, a gathering of African American men in Washington, D.C. Numerous civil rights organizations participated in the march, along with thousands of Black men throughout the country.

Editors at the *Tennessean* were not in favor of having a reporter ride a bus with the march participants from Nashville, saying the march was not a big deal. The editorial team published a column by conservative

Cal Thomas saying that Farrakhan "wasn't a good role model" for Black people.

Bridges was furious. "There was a big fight in the newsroom," Bridges recalled. In the end, reporter Wendy Thomas decided on her own to ride one of the buses. Between that and the palpable newsroom disappointment at the O. J. Simpson verdict, Bridges knew it was time to go.

After leaving the *Tennessean*, Bridges landed in Newport News, Virginia, as a team leader at the *Daily Press* for two years before joining the Virginia Press Association in Richmond as its professional development director, a job that harkened back to her days at the Maynard Institute. After a six-year stretch at VPA, Bridges returned to a world that jump-started her career nearly four decades earlier: the daily newsroom.

In 2005, she was hired at the *Virginian-Pilot* in Norfolk, Virginia, as director of recruitment and staff development, a job that she could shape into her own, and she "finally found a husband to keep."

Bridges stayed at the *Pilot* until newspaper layoffs swept the country and finally landed on her doorstep on December 20, 2013.

"I left not wanting to leave," she said, but Bridges had observed many rounds of layoffs at the newspaper, so she was not surprised when it was her turn to say goodbye.

When asked about the lows of being a Black woman in the news industry, Bridges equates them to being in a war zone.

"The lows are always related to having to fight some battles and defend the craft," she said during a 2015 interview. "To me these were the frustrating things. Then you realize people are ingrained in their thinking.

"Things just haven't changed as much as you would think after forty years. It's still not fair coverage that is striking the right tone. Look at Baltimore," she said, referring to the Freddie Gray incident that occurred on April 12, 2015, when 25-year-old Freddie Carlos Gray Jr. died after being arrested by the Baltimore Police Department for possessing a knife. As he was transported in a police van, Gray sustained injuries and was taken to the R Adams Cowley Shock Trauma Center at the University of

Maryland Medical Center. He died on April 19, 2015, reportedly from injuries to his spinal cord.

"It's still stereotypical stupid coverage," said Bridges. "I'm not saying these things didn't happen, but put them in context."

She is hopeful that journalism will attract young people who aren't afraid to ask the hard questions and "get back to reporting objectively and respecting the craft. If we do that, we demonstrate to people the importance of supporting local journalism, because it's central to our democracy."

Chapter 2

Fannie Flono

Curiosity and Persistence Propel Her Career—Words as Weapons for Slaying

Fannie Flono was a high school senior when Black residents in her hometown of Augusta, Georgia—grown weary by the city's racist treatment of them—struck back. On May 11, 1970, more than one hundred blocks of neighborhoods and businesses—about seven miles—were ransacked and vandalized by Blacks protesting the death of 16-year-old Charles Oatman, who died in the Richmond County jail on May 9, 1970, according to an October 2020 NPR report.

Described as intellectually disabled and weighing about a hundred pounds, many said Oatman should have been in the area's juvenile detention center for his crime, which was the accidental shooting death of his 5-year-old niece. Placed in jail without bond, Oatman died six weeks later, his body bearing brutal gashes and a busted skull. In the ensuing violent protests, police killed six Black men and injured several others.

Flono, who retired as an associate editor, columnist, and editorial writer from the *Charlotte Observer's* editorial board in 2014, was among the protesters, as an observer.

"People were rampaging and tearing up cars," she recalled. "We were warning drivers where they shouldn't go because people were being beaten and robbed" following the initial protests.

Flono's presence did not go undetected. Watching the riots on television were her parents, Adam Flono, a Bell Telephone lineman, and Prudence Flono, a domestic worker who taught her children how to read when they were 3 and 4 years old.

"She can't be in the middle of the riots," the couple told one another.

Whether or not they were surprised by their daughter's actions, the Flonos knew that she was doing what they had long encouraged their offspring to do to "understand the world around us."

For Fannie Flono, understanding the world started with reading newspapers, writing poetry, and working for her John M. Tutt High School newspaper. Her knowledge of Black history, civil rights, and racial injustice was amplified "after reading *Black Rage, Soul on Ice,* and other books during my high school years that illuminated Black justice issues. The riots didn't spark my activism; that fire had already been lit by my parents, by my reading, and my observations of the racism and political machinations in my hometown and state. But the riots were a reminder and prod that active work against injustice was always necessary for change."

Despite her thirst for activism and news, Flono was unsure of her career path when she enrolled at Clark Atlanta University five months after the May riots. However, once she switched her major from psychology to English and language, her future became more focused.

"I thought that I'd one day write the great American novel. Even when I switched to English, I didn't know what I'd do with it. In college, I was involved in women's issues and social justice issues."

A professor suggested that Flono consider journalism. She became an intern for the *Macon Telegraph*.

What did her professor see in her that stood out?

"That I was active and I worked for the school newspaper," said Flono. She'd written about two white students (who were enrolled at the historically Black Clark Atlanta). One wanted to play football, and the other student wanted to study African American history.

The internship was the encouragement Flono needed to pursue journalism.

"I had a great time ... to see my name on the front page, and I was still a student! It was head turning, even for a small-town newspaper."

Flono's sense of curiosity also played a role in her swift ascent into a field where Black journalists— particularly Black women—were not the norm. She also relished the opportunity to shape an industry where news coverage often was skewed. During the riots she witnessed before coming to college, she believed that the stories being told "weren't true to the experiences I saw—that Black people weren't caricatures, criminals, or didn't have aspirations for different kinds of lives."

After college, Flono was hired as the education and police reporter in Lakeland, Florida, where she stayed for seven months between 1974 and 1975.

One of her first assignments was to cover a Ku Klux Klan parade, which she described as an "out-of-body experience. They were spouting out all these things about Black people [but] being nice to me, as if I wasn't Black."

Flono, surprised that KKK parades still occurred, said it attracted crowds. "They [KKK members] were in their full regalia. It was very weird. I interviewed the KKK leader. He didn't seem to feel it was unusual about a Black person interviewing him. I was like, 'How can you talk to me so calmly when you hate Black people?' I just found it weird. He invited me to one of their night meetings. I wanted to go, but my editor and photographer felt that wouldn't be a good idea." While in Lakeland, Flono received hate mail and hate calls because her newspaper column ran with her photo. Callers harassed her, and she received death threats. Her parents told her to go to the NAACP.

"I still have letters where they [readers] referred to Blacks as *coons*," Flono said.

The job was an eye-opener, and she is fond of telling young reporters, "Listen, you can work anywhere for seven months because I did."

She became uneasy about being there, and eventually left for a job as the health, education, police, and courts reporter for the *Columbus (GA) Enquirer*.

Before she arrived at the paper in 1975, she received a letter that said, "We do not hire Blacks. Where did you get our address?" Flono was stunned.

"That was the first time I ever got a letter like that; it was really hurtful. The letter was a really angry letter."

By the time Flono started working in Columbus, Knight Ridder had purchased the newspaper, but the climate of the place wasn't much different from the tone of the letter. A colleague who sat behind her would make phone calls and refer to her as a "nigger."

This is where Flono's soft-spoken, friendly manner became the polar opposite.

"I walked out and said I'd come back when they made him stop the harassment. They threatened to fire him, which made him stop. He apparently was not liked by a lot of people."

Even as a police reporter, Flono endured harassment by Black and white police officers who tried to "hit on me." She told the police chief who reined them in. "They grew up thinking Black women were loose."

After nearly four years in Columbus, Flono left the newspaper in 1978 to enroll in graduate school at the University of South Carolina. A stint at the *Augusta Chronicle* for nine months in 1979 was followed by a position as wire editor at the *Greenville (SC) Piedmont* from 1981 to 1983. "The job was interesting because it meant culling all sorts of news stories." Flono then spent a year, from 1983 to 1984, as an assistant city editor at the *Greenville News*.

When Flono received a call from Al Johnson, a Black editor with the *Charlotte (NC) Observer*, she prepared for her next move. It was a game of cat and mouse: the paper wanted to hire her; the paper didn't want to hire her.

One of the editors said Flono "thought too much of myself." When she arrived at the paper, she intended to be there five years at best. She stayed an additional twenty-five years. Around the time Flono arrived in Charlotte in 1984 as an assistant state editor, the city was trying to carve a more polished identity separate from its Southern, race car–driving roots. Its daily newspaper, the *Charlotte Observer*, also wanted a newsroom that reflected the city's growing diversity and reputation for attracting corporations and new industries. Under the leadership of people such as Johnson, who is credited with expanding the newspaper's regional footprint in the 1980s, and Flono, the paper's rebranding was unfolding.

"We never [Blacks] outnumbered whites, but we had a significant number of Black people," said Flono. "We were significant enough to start an NABJ chapter. One editor thought that NABJ was a union, that we were showing favoritism to Blacks. He ordered us not to do it. He also told me not to have lunch with Black people only. I asked him, 'Why not?'"

Flono was not the easiest person to supervise because "whenever someone tells me what to do, I want to know why." She and the editor had to go through counseling. "It was almost like marriage counseling; he was probably twenty years older."

Flono had no qualms about acting on and voicing the fears of every white newsroom supervisor or editor. She let it be known that anytime she was treated unfairly she would take the newspaper to court, and that it would be a "long and messy" proceeding.

As for the editor with whom she underwent counseling, she said they ultimately agreed to disagree. Meanwhile, Flono went on to serve in several management positions at the paper, including assistant government and political editor, night metro editor, metro/city editor, public editor, and from 1993 to 2014, associate editor, columnist, and editorial writer.

Truth Tellers: *The Power and Presence of Black Women Journalists Since 1960*

Flono never spent much time thinking about her status as the first Black woman to be an associate editor on the *Charlotte Observer*'s editorial board or to serve in other leadership positions. She simply found her work interesting and enjoyed encouraging people to write about the community.

Her plainspoken manner was not lost on readers, whether she was writing about white Appalachians who planned to vote for Barack Obama in 2008 but still referred to him as an N-word; struggling schools; corporate executives' lavish spending on resorts, golf, and spas during a recession; or the haunting atrocities of Vietnam decades after the war ended.

A June 7, 2012 headline on an article in the *Columbia Journalism Review* described Flono as "a conversation convener" with the subhead "Fannie Flono, *Charlotte Observer* Columnist and 'Sassy Black Woman,' Talks About Her Public Consideration of Ideas."

Although the subhead echoed Flono's recollection of one hiring editor's remark that she "thought too much of herself" and the stereotypical "sassy" Black woman trope, Flono was clear in defining her role to *CJR*, a news industry publication.

"My perch at the paper provided a platform to get public consideration of ideas and ways of thinking about issues they may not have considered. I also saw my role as helping people bridge gaps in understanding, finding a way to reach consensus, to be less myopic, and to have a broader lens to discuss issues and make decisions."

Flono's *Charlotte Observer* column ran in other McClatchy newspapers as well as in other North Carolina papers, such as the *Winston-Salem Journal*, the *Greensboro News & Record*, and the *Burlington Times-News*. Also, as a 1998-99 Nieman Fellow at Harvard University, she studied the impact of race and class on public school education and has traveled on fellowships to Japan, South Korea, China, and Germany. She also was a fellow with the Institute for Educational Inquiry in Seattle, Washington.

As a consultant for the Kettering Foundation, a national nonpartisan think tank based in Dayton, Ohio, that fosters public dialogue and community engagement, Flono has written several booklets about education and race. In 2006, she wrote *Thriving in the Shadows: The Black Experience in Charlotte and Mecklenburg County,* and is published in the 2014 anthology *27 Views of Charlotte: The Queen City in Prose and Poetry.*

Flono was inducted into the Charlotte Women's History Hall of Fame, has received the Maya Angelou Women Who Lead Award, and the Charlotte YWCA Women of Achievement Pioneer Award. She serves on the boards of Read Charlotte and the Charlotte Museum of History, where she chairs its efforts to Save the Siloam School, a Rosenwald school and National Historic Landmarks site.

She said the yearlong Nieman stay at Harvard University "was like a breath of fresh air" and came when she needed a break "to rediscover me. . .to do the things I wanted to do for me and not doing it for someone else." Flono also is grateful for the lifelong friends she met at Harvard.

When Flono retired, it probably was then that the magnitude of her life's work hit her. "There were many who talked about how I opened the door for them. My siblings had always said that I didn't realize the importance of my work. They always thought that it was kind of cool."

Years after retiring from the *Observer*, Flono, who enjoyed seeing celebrities who came to the newsroom, still speaks passionately about newspapers having succumbed to too much entertainment.

"I made my peace with those kinds of changes a long time ago," Flono said in 2015 during a luncheon meeting in SouthPark, a trendy hotspot for Charlotte's professional workers. "As a onetime political editor, I used to relish the competition—the deeper, richer knowledge that such coverage can bring. Today, there's a lot that goes unpublished. But, all in all, we still do a lot of good stuff."

Flono's advice for women entering the field is simple: "Know what you want and go after it ferociously. I was very passionate about my career.

"Be prepared for opportunities," she added, recalling her message one year to graduates at Charlotte's Johnson C. Smith University, a private historically Black university. "You only get one life. There are no do-overs if you don't do the things that you want to do in order to give your life purpose."

Flono still thinks about the young woman who wanted to write the great American novel. But she's comfortable knowing that her work as a journalist is equally significant.

"I'm happy that people think I've made an impact to the extent that people tell me I've done that."

Chapter 3

Norma Adams-Wade

Just the Facts, Please—Recording Momentous Hometown History for Fifty Years

When Norma Adams-Wade arrived at the University of Texas at Austin in 1962, America's civil rights movement was constantly in the news. On June 11, 1963, shortly after her freshman year had ended, Alabama governor George C. Wallace physically blocked two Black students from registering at the University of Alabama in Tuscaloosa. He didn't back down until President John F. Kennedy sent the National Guard to the campus.

On August 28, 1963, approximately 250,000 people participating in the March on Washington for Jobs and Freedom heard the Reverend Dr. Martin Luther King Jr. deliver his "I Have A Dream" speech in front of the Lincoln Memorial.

"I have a dream that one day this nation will rise up and live out the true meaning of its creed: 'We hold these truths to be self-evident: that all men are created equal.'"

Less than a month later, on September 15, 1963, a bomb at 16th Street Baptist Church in Birmingham, Alabama, killed four young girls and injured several other people prior to Sunday services. Angry protests followed.

And, on November 22, 1963, as Adams-Wade walked toward her co-op housing building at UT-Austin, she noticed people frantically running through campus. When she reached her destination, she walked inside to see pandemonium. Several students were glued to the television, crying. President Kennedy had been killed while riding in a motorcade in downtown Dallas, her hometown.

Norma Adams Wade's high school graduation photo circa early 1960s.

"I don't remember crying, but I remember that I felt as if I'd been sucker punched," she said. "I hung around downstairs, and then I went to my room. I may have started writing about what happened because that's what I do. I put together my thoughts, but just for myself. At some point, I called home and spoke to my dad. We just talked about all that was going on in terms of news coverage at home. I remember Walter Cronkite of CBS on the news talking all the time. I remember the TV screens being blank at times. Nobody else I've talked to seems to remember that black out. I do not believe I imagined it."

Although Adams-Wade wrote about the assassination, she never published a story about that fateful day. It was her habit, she said, always to be an observer and to take notes.

Amid all the chaos of the era, "my counterparts were very up front in the protest movement--protesting and marching," she recalled. "I would be on the scene. I always viewed myself as a record keeper. I was interested and impressed with the potential progress being made. I was a bit fearful for the safety of my friends who were more aggressive. It all just fascinated me because it was a fascinating development in life. I was curious to see where it all was headed."

Petite and plainspoken, Adams-Wade insists that her life story, set in one of America's largest cities that once was the name of a popular television series, is "nothing sexy."

Not that she dismisses her career that enabled her to meet and interview practically any prominent African American who came to Dallas, including Alex Haley, the author of *Roots*, whom she especially enjoyed interviewing. Rather, her life's work is simply a manifestation of a "very quiet and patterned" childhood involving her parents, Frank M. Adams and Nettie Ruth Ivory Adams, and an older sister, Doris Crawford Adams Serrell. Besides her family, religion and reading were her constant companions as a youngster.

Adams-Wade's penchant for powerful language and writing was honed in elementary school by libraries, books, and storytelling that exposed her to worlds beyond her small, quiet working-class community in South Dallas. "I fell in love with books in the third grade. I was taken away by *Robinson Crusoe* and *Treasure Island* and being on an exotic island. That led to bringing home from the city library arm loads of books—twenty to thirty—that I would read in short order. I lived all of that . . . skating in New York, wagon trains in the 1800s. That was my life. Those pages of those books gave me so much pleasure."

An accomplished singer and pianist, Adams-Wade was encouraged to study and pursue a career in fine arts. But journalism had already struck a chord with her, heightened by a Black woman journalist who was a guest speaker at an elementary school program. Julia Scott Reed, an impressive woman who wrote for the local Black newspaper and was a self-taught radio announcer, photographer and soon newspaper managing editor, remained a career touchstone. "I didn't know Black people wrote for newspapers," Adams-Wade remembered thinking at the time.

Adams-Wade's father read *The Dallas Morning News* from cover to cover each day, a ritual that also fueled her fascination with journalism. When she graduated from Lincoln High School in 1962 and enrolled at the UT-Austin, her goal was to work her way back home and write for *The Dallas Morning News*.

"So that was always the route, to end up at the paper that I had seen my dad read my whole life," she said.

Her father's postal worker salary paid for her tuition at UT-Austin. Adams-Wade said that while there, she was among Black student "test guinea pigs" for the university's experiment with integrated co-op houses and dormitories. She said all the young women in her first-time integrated co-op house—ironically named Whitis—"got along famously in a beautiful turn-of-the-century house. ...I fell in love with big wrap-around porches."

Other than the Kennedy assassination, Adams-Wade described college life as wonderful but uneventful. Of course, there was the infamous August 1, 1966 tower shooting the summer after Adams-Wade graduated. Gunman Charles Whitman killed 15 people and injured many others. Also, there is the fact that President Lyndon Johnson spoke at Adams-Wade's graduation because his daughter, Lynda Bird Johnson, was in Adams-Wade's same graduating class. Adams-Wade wrote for her college newspaper, the *Daily Texan*, and recalled one petite but stern female professor who had been a military officer.

"Professor Mary Gardner was a stickler for accuracy, proper English, grammar, and spelling. If you misspelled one word on a test, you would get an F," said Adams-Wade. "She was not playing."

If any racially charged incidents were aimed at Adams-Wade during her four years at UT and later during her career, she said she simply "kept it moving." Even interviewing members of the Ku Klux Klan when she reported for *The Dallas Morning News* didn't bother her.

"There were KKK marches from time to time with me being the observer or interviewer with a notebook and pen. It was just a fascinating conversation to have with another human being who looked at life differently. Their personal attitudes didn't get to me. I just felt they were unfortunate. Overall, I was fairly well-received. I could hang with anybody."

After graduating in 1966 from UT-Austin, Adams-Wade returned home and interviewed with *The Dallas Morning News*. She entered the newsroom and saw her longtime idol, Julia Scott Reed, seated prominently in the front of the newsroom. For Adams-Wade, Reed's positioning served two purposes: *The Dallas Morning News* wanted everyone to know that it was a racially integrated newsroom and that, even though Reed was the only Black woman working there, they had their quota. Adams-Wade was not hired. Instead, she went to work at Texas Instruments where she edited NASA's technical manuals for space-tracking devices. She eventually left the company to work for Bloom Advertising in its trafficking division and later began editing ads for the company. She quit after being informed that one of the white male editors said that he did not want a Black person on his team. Wade, then a newlywed, said the incident occurred around the same time that civil rights leader Dr. King was assassinated on April 4, 1968, in Memphis, Tennessee.

"I remember saying I can't make myself go back. I did not go back." Instead, she returned to the *Dallas Post Tribune*, a Black newspaper where she had held summer internships while in college. Hired as assistant to Dickie Foster, the paper's editor, Adams-Wade led a redesign of the production process to help the organization run more smoothly.

While working for the *Dallas Post Tribune*, Adams-Wade was approached by R. E. "Buster" Haas, then city editor for *The Dallas Morning News*, who would later serve as assistant managing editor. He came to her home and asked her to write a freelance story that resulted in a banner headline.

In 1974, nearly eight years after she graduated from the UT-Austin, Adams-Wade's determination to present Dallas's Black communities and residents in a more positive light was realized. She became the first full-time African American general assignment reporter for *The Dallas Morning News*.

Her desire to write for *The Dallas Morning News* was fueled while growing up in the North Texas city during the 1940s and 1950s when de facto segregation was the norm. Back then, Adams-Wade said she rarely saw stories about The Dallas she knew, where Black people lived, worked, played and prayed together.

"Dallas was a racist town," she recalled. "But we knew how to live our lives. Weekends you'd catch the bus downtown to the five-and-dime store, H. L. Green, an economical, one-stop shopping place on a downtown bus line where Blacks and whites gathered. Blacks congregated among ourselves, whether it was church, stores or recreation. Blacks had our own YMCAs or YWCAs and movie theaters. Dallas was segregated and racist, but we lived our own lives in our own ways."

Shortly after arriving at *The Dallas Morning News*, Adams-Wade's world expanded even more. Chuck Stone, a reporter and columnist for the *Philadelphia Daily News*, notified newsrooms throughout the country about a new organization formed by and for Black journalists. Adams-Wade's editor gave her a copy of Stone's letter and "he had me from 'hello,'" she recalled. Adams-Wade traveled to the meeting that took place on December 12, 1975, in Washington, D.C.'s Sheraton Park Hotel. She was so excited that she paid for the trip herself; it was well worth the cost to meet dozens of journalists from throughout the country, most of whom were the only Black staffer in their newsrooms.

"It was like a church revival, knowing there were others like me in newsrooms in other parts of the country," said Adams-Wade. "The adrenalin was flowing . . . to be congregated with others who had the same experiences. Up until then, going to church on weekends was where I got my rejuvenation."

Stone led the meeting that culminated with the formation of the National Association of Black Journalists, combining several independent associations in cities such as Chicago, San Francisco, Philadelphia, and Washington, D.C., according to *Black Journalists: The NABJ Story*, by

Norma Adams Wade

Norma Adams Wade speaks at a community event in the late 1980s.

Wayne Dawkins. Adams-Wade not only became one of the organization's forty-four founding members, but was tapped as the first regional director for five states, including Dallas. NABJ's mission sought to strengthen ties among Black journalists, sensitize media to fairness in the workplace for Black journalists, and expand job opportunities for veteran, young, and aspiring journalists, along with providing professional development and training. Adams-Wade returned to Dallas with renewed zeal about her role as a Black journalist and as one who viewed herself as a modern-day African griot.

In 1979, a few years after becoming involved in NABJ, Adams-Wade was invited to join the editing staff for the Maynard Institute for Journalism Education in Berkeley, California. The program was created by Robert "Bob" Maynard, publisher of the *Oakland Tribune*; his wife, Nancy Hicks Maynard; and several other minority journalists. Its purpose was to ensure that the nation's news media reflected diversity in staffing, content, and business operations. Adams-Wade gained the support of her editors to work with the program that summer. Divorced by then, she brought along her then 5-year-old daughter, Amber Akili, and hired a sitter to stay with her while Adams-Wade helped train student journalists during the day. She returned to assist in the summer training program in 1994 when it was held in Tucson, Arizona.

Adams-Wade retired from *The Dallas Morning News* in 2002. She had covered federal courts, general assignments, consumer affairs and, in 1988 began writing a weekly column that she continues to write while retired. She also writes for other Dallas-based news publications, including a weekly column that runs in three Black-owned newspapers: *Texas Metro News, Garland Journals,* and the digital *I Messenger Media.* Her achievements and work have been recognized with awards that include the Press Club of Dallas' Excellence in Journalism: North Texas Legends Awards, The Dallas Fort-Worth Association of Black Journalists Lifetime Achievement Award, and the Norma Adams-Wade NABJ Founders Scholarship.

Another reason that Adams-Wade never left Dallas is because of the words former Illinois Governor Adlai Stevenson II relayed in a speech to a university graduating class: "'When you leave, don't forget why you came.' Over the years at *The Dallas Morning News*, I could not forget why I came," Adams-Wade said.

Some of her recent columns have drawn similarities between America's racist past and the uproar after the death of George Floyd, an African American man. Floyd was choked to death in Minneapolis on May 25, 2020 by white police officer Derek Chauvin. Floyd died handcuffed and prone on the ground while Chauvin pressed his knee on Floyd's neck for 9 minutes, 29 seconds.

Now, as then, Adams-Wade continues to pepper her prose with words that spell truth. "Civil rights leaders in the 1960s called the chaos 'rebellions, civil unrest or disorders,'" Adams-Wade wrote in a June 2, 2020 column in *The Dallas Morning News*. "People in the news media called them 'riots.' Whatever your description, the maddening conflicts have returned in 2020 with the same fury and frustration and ignited by the same fuel—police brutality, social and economic inequality, and the hopelessness of poverty."

Adams-Wade's columns about George Floyd, all these years later, could have been written during any decade of her youth. "*The twains of the have and have-nots, Blacks and whites, privileged and oppressed still vow to never meet. Communities of color still rage against police officers while police supporters still hurl back invectives that officers are 'just doing their job.'"*

In telling the stories of Black folks, whether covering their communities or covering Black defendants in federal court, Adams-Wade always strove for balance, fairness, and sensitivity in her coverage. An example of her determination to highlight positive stories was further realized in 1985 when she created a Black history series about notable African Americans that were featured every day in February.

Such a body of work is why Adams-Wade continues to focus on Dallas' African American communities with residents who still lament the closing of the historically Black Bishop College in 1988, and witness the gentrification unfolding daily in the Bonton neighborhood where she grew up.

"Remembering why I came kept me writing as a reporter instead of moving up as an editor or leaving for another city. So, leaving town? Never much considered it. My 'calling' was here. My hometown. I still enjoy it. And I am still committed."

Chapter 4

Dorothy Butler Gilliam

A Legendary Trailblazer and Pioneer—From Alienation to Spiritual Leadership

By Janet Davenport

When Dorothy Butler Gilliam stepped onto Black Lives Matter Plaza in Washington, D.C., on a bright summer morning in 2020, it was a transcendent moment for the journalism legend. "It felt as if I was stepping on holy ground," Gilliam said, recalling the visit she made for the first time to the transformed two-block section of 16th Street, NW, across from the White House.

Like many Americans, Gilliam was just beginning to venture outside her home, taking precautions such as wearing a face mask, as cities gradually reopened businesses and loosened restrictions imposed by the COVID-19 pandemic.

Mayor Muriel Bowser renamed the plaza after the Public Works Department painted "Black Lives Matter" in giant letters on the street in a show of support for the national protests that started in Minneapolis in response to the killing of George Floyd, a 46-year-old unarmed Black man, during an arrest on May 25, 2020. Almost six decades earlier, at the tender age of 23, with a master's degree from Columbia University, Gilliam stepped into the newsroom of the *Washington Post* to become the first Black woman, and the second African American to be hired as a reporter at the venerable newspaper.

Gilliam, an award-winning journalist who sharpened her reporting and writing skills in high school and then college working for the *Black Press*, blazed trails in and out of the newsroom. She paid dearly for her pioneering efforts, which she chronicles in her 2019 memoir *Trailblazer: A Pioneering Journalist's Fight to Make the Media Look More Like America*. With clarity and candor, she reveals the isolation and humiliation she endured—and the anxiety and the depression she battled to build her venerable career.

Many of her white colleagues, including other women also breaking new professional ground, alienated her. Taxicabs would not stop for her. When she showed up for assignments, white and Black Washingtonians questioned her press credentials. In retrospect, Gilliam calls her initial professional expectations as "naive" as she went on to break color and gender barriers in the newsroom.

"Starting out, I was much more conservative. I didn't want to cover Black stories. I just wanted to cover news stories fairly and accurately," Gilliam said. However, endowed with a keen appreciation not only for history but also for her place in it, Gilliam eventually decided during her early years at the *Post* that she would be intentional about bringing a Black woman's perspective to the news and issues of the day and to shining a light on Black life and the Black community.

"I came to realize that as a Black woman I could bring a perspective and understanding of my culture that would be of value in the mainstream news industry," she said. "Being the first in a segregated city and swimming in a sea of white men, not getting taxicabs, not getting hotel rooms, forced to sleep in a funeral home took a toll."

Gilliam says she finally realized that journalism inherently required emotional suppression because of its constantly changing, fast pace. "I was under a lot of emotional stress, and I did not realize just how much at the time. My ex-husband told me years later, 'You weren't aware of the bondage' you were under." It was the sixties, which many historians describe as the most turbulent decade in American history. Everything was changing. Gilliam, a "PK" (preacher's kid) and a daughter of the Jim Crow South, could not have known what a prominent role she would play in changing the complexion of the newsroom, a bastion of white male supremacy.

Born in 1936 in Memphis, Tennessee, Gilliam was the eighth of ten children, and one of only five to reach adulthood. Her parents, Adee Conklin Butler and Jessie Mae Norment Butler, moved their brood to Louisville, Kentucky, when her father was appointed pastor of a new African Methodist Episcopal congregation. Gilliam excelled academically, winning admission to a private Catholic high school and graduating with honors from Lincoln University, a historically Black college in Pennsylvania. She wrote for *Jet* and *Ebony* magazines and decided to apply to Columbia University when white-owned, mainstream dailies did not respond to her inquiries. When she landed at the *Washington Post*, Gilliam was forced to navigate racism in the newsroom and in Washington, but found the courage of her convictions to cover major historic events during the civil rights era.

As a reporter, she traveled to Mississippi in 1962 to cover the integration of the University of Mississippi. She narrowly escaped a potentially dangerous encounter with a gang of gun-toting white men. Later, unable to get a hotel room in town, she slept at a Black-owned funeral parlor. However, she recognized how much worse it could have been, recalling in her memoir how her early mentor and dear friend, L. Allen Wilson of the *Tri-State Defender*, was attacked by a mob of whites and nearly beaten to death when he covered school integration in Little Rock, Arkansas.

"My purpose changed," Gilliam said. "And I feel that in writing so much about the Black community, I fulfilled my purpose," she said, noting that she faced criticism for that, too. People complained, "All you write about is race," she said.

The intrepid Gilliam would become an editor and popular columnist for the *Washington Post* before retiring in 2003, leaving a huge imprint on the profession and the American journalism landscape. Her credits and accolades are legendary and lengthy. To mention a few: She co-founded and served on the board of the Robert C. Maynard Institute for Journalism Education; she served as the president of the National Association of Black Journalists and of the Unity of Journalists of Color. Gilliam was a leader of the first Unity Convention held in 1994 when an estimated 8,000 journalists of color converged in Atlanta, Georgia, to address ongoing concerns of inclusion and diversity in American newsrooms and coverage of Black, Hispanic, Native American, and Asian communities.

Dorothy Butler Gilliam at her desk in late 1961 or early 1962 at The Washington Post. (Copyright, Harry Naltchayan, The Washington Post.)

Truth Tellers: *The Power and Presence of Black Women Journalists Since 1960*

She has mentored and trained thousands of journalists of color, not just for print but also for television and new media platforms. Yet, to the consternation of her editors, Gilliam quit the *Washington Post* in 1967. "It was just too much," she said, explaining that she was pregnant with her third child. The paper rehired her in 1972, which she said marked the beginning of her "spiritual" reawakening. "I realized that even with my deep, strong upbringing as a PK, I had drifted away," she said. She befriended a woman from Trinidad, a temporary employee at the *Post*, who invited her to a brunch.

She arrived at the gathering to find a group of women seated on the floor talking about spirituality, faith, and healings. "Their faith seemed so real and vibrant," Gilliam said. Her friend established a regular prayer network that became an invaluable support system and source of inspiration as she faced the challenges of balancing family and journalism. "Meeting hatred with love, learning to live and triumph in the midst of oppression, this is how we [Black people] have survived 400 years."

"Even when we did not name it, we understood this hope and faith built into our psyche from the beginning," Gilliam said. Describing her life as a "spiritual journey," over time she has come to understand that it was the faith and resiliency she inherited from her strong Black family and community that sustained and propelled her all along. Visiting the Black Lives Matter Plaza at the invitation of one of her young mentees reminded her of that foundation, and the history she has lived, witnessed, and recorded.

The visit also provided a glimpse of the future. Gilliam liked what she saw. "I was surprised," she said, recounting the scene through the clarity of a reporter's lens: *It was early and quiet. Empty vending tables were around. The Black Lives Matter sign was huge in the middle of the street, throwing distance from the White House. BLM murals were posted on the fence, and painted on the panels of boarded-up buildings, the police surrounding the area so the only access was by foot.*

"There is a stronger sense of people coming together from different racial, income, and faith backgrounds. There is a fearlessness. Hatemongers are trying to denigrate the BLM movement and antiracist protestors, but they're saying *we're not scared*."

Gilliam, 86, said she felt a sense of pride and hope walking along Black Lives Matter Plaza. The stillness of the early morning hour allowed her to bear witness to a significant moment in American history and to savor the intersections with her spiritual journey as a Black woman, a journalist, and a trailblazer.

Janet Davenport helps changemakers lead and communicate from the power of their passion and purpose through her firm, Davenport Coaching Solutions. A seasoned journalist, Davenport is a former editorial writer and editorial board member of the Hartford Courant (CT), and a former editorial page editor, reporter, and feature writer for the Republican in Springfield, Massachusetts.

Chapter 5

Robin Farmer

A Witness to the Truth—A Clear-Eyed Childhood
Scripted Her Future

Robin Farmer's interest in journalism was sparked by a news industry legend who worked in her hometown: Chuck Stone, the renowned columnist for the *Philadelphia Daily News*.

His column was called And the Angels Sing, and Stone often used his position as the newspaper's first Black writer and editor to call out racism, political corruption, and police brutality, particularly against African Americans. His influence was so wide- ranging that alleged criminals routinely surrendered to Stone for him to document their physical condition prior to their incarceration.

Reading his column was like listening to the "angels sing," said the effusive Farmer about Stone. "Here's the beauty of Chuck Stone: Stone was so good he would give haters a verbal beat down, and they wouldn't know it. I read his columns with a dictionary, which I loved."

Inspired by journalists such as Stone and others whose prose still speaks to her heart, Farmer spent nearly twenty-five years working as a journalist in Richmond, Virginia, and Hartford, Connecticut. The recipient of numerous honors and awards, she is now a freelance writer whose work has appeared in the *Washington Post*, theroot.com, *Richmond Magazine*, and *Black MBA Magazine*. Her debut novel, *Malcolm and Me*, was published in November 2020. Met with favorable reviews, Amazon described the book as "a gritty yet graceful examination of the anguish teens experience when their growing awareness of themselves and the world around them unravels their sense of security—a coming-of-age tale of truth-telling, faith, family, forgiveness, and social activism."

Farmer's interest in writing formed as a young child.

"I loved to read and write since age 4," said Farmer, who specialized in education coverage while in Richmond. "When I read, I traveled the world."

Farmer decided at age 7 that she someday would write full time. By 11, her interest in truth telling and addressing powerful people and institutions took root when her sixth-grade Catholic school teacher asked her why Thomas Jefferson owned slaves as a signer of the Declaration of Independence.

Farmer replied that he was a "hypocrite." Angered by Farmer's outburst, the teacher told Farmer to "get on a boat and go back to Africa."

The incident still resonates with Farmer today. "I was 11 when I saw racism and religion collide."

Armed with a new sense of empowerment bolstered by an affinity for comic book reporter Brenda Starr, teen detective fictional character Nancy Drew, and political activist Angela Davis, Farmer pursued her dreams of writing to eventually see her photo in *Right On* magazine, a beloved teen publication created in 1971. Cynthia Horner, the magazine's editor, encouraged Farmer to keep writing after she tied for first place in the magazine's first national Black history awareness contest.

Truth Tellers: *The Power and Presence of Black Women Journalists Since 1960*

After her *Right On* experience, Farmer set her sights on television directing and participated in a program for high school students from 1975 to 1978 that exposed them to behind-the-camera positions. She later became the youngest talk show associate producer at KYW TV-3.

After high school, she enrolled in Marquette University and majored in journalism with a minor in film. Working for Marquette's student newspaper, radio station, and handling public relations assignments gave Farmer the skills to assume her first job after graduation—working for Wilson Goode, Sr., Philadelphia's first Black mayor. Goode hired Farmer because she impressed him with her work on his mayoral campaign.

"I was one of 10,000 volunteers on his campaign. He hired me on the spot because I could write a press release," she said.

Although she enjoyed working in the mayor's office, the ever-observant Farmer took mental notes each time the news media showed up. The mayor's staff sat on one side of the table while the press sat on the opposite side. Farmer, who longed to become a newspaper journalist, decided that she wanted to be on the side with the news media.

"I wanted to help write a page of Philadelphia history by helping to get Mayor Goode elected. But I always knew I wanted to go back to my first love, which was newspaper reporting."

Farmer's decision led to her selection for the acclaimed Summer Program for Minority Journalists at the University of California, Berkeley. After completing the program, she went to the *Hartford Courant* and stayed there for seventeen months. A call from Earle Dunford, city editor of the *Richmond Times-Dispatch*, lured her to the South.

Farmer arrived in Richmond, Virginia, the former capital of the Confederacy, in 1988 where she bloomed where rooted. She quickly carved out a reputation as an award-winning journalist, serving on the paper's investigative team, writing about education, Confederate flags, Black youths in peril, and occasionally writing film and concert reviews.

Highlights from her twenty-one-year career at the *Times-Dispatch*, as its staffers referred to the paper once owned by Media General Inc.

and for several years was part of Warren Buffet's Berkshire Hathaway news group, are many, said Farmer. One assignment included teaching at a middle school for a semester to gain a better understanding of how the school system operated.

"Those kids did something to my heart," she said about the experience. "It was an eye-opener."

Farmer, who served as the president of the Education Writers Association, decided to do the project to help readers understand the challenges teachers face every day in urban schools. Her series "Trading Places: From the Newsroom to the Classroom" won a national first-place award.

Farmer left the *T-D* in 2009 during a massive layoff involving sixty employees. At the time, such layoffs were not unusual in the newspaper industry, which was bleeding from decreased circulation, buyouts, and emerging digital media. The *Richmond Times-Dispatch*, which had merged with the *Richmond News Leader*, its sister afternoon paper, in the early 1990s, was sold to Lee Industries in January 2020.

Overall, Farmer's newspaper journalism career included more highs than lows. Her award-winning work on the investigative team led to her selection as a fellow at the University of Michigan, another career high.

"My fellowship at the University of Michigan validated that I could run with the big boys in journalism since only twelve journalists are selected both nationally and globally."

Further validation of what it means to be a caring and passionate writer while also being the supportive wife of a journalist came in June 2021. Farmer's husband, Michael Paul Williams, a longtime columnist for the *Richmond Times-Dispatch*, was awarded the 2021 Pulitzer Prize for Commentary for his "penetrating and insightful columns that led Richmond, a former capital of the Confederacy, through the painful and complicated process of dismantling the city's monuments to white supremacy."

"I am beyond elated," Farmer said of her and her husband's achievements.

PART 2

From Setbacks to Success

Chapter 6

Lynne K. Varner

Unheeding the Headwinds—Crafting a Career with Intention and Purpose

By Cathy Gant Hill

Several minutes into a discussion about her career, Lynne K. Varner is talking and talking ... about other people and *their* talents:

What a brilliant journalist Gwen Ifill was. How the legendary Helen Thomas would dictate nearly seamless copy to Varner in the UPI newsroom from Air Force One. What a discerning and gifted storyteller is newswoman Michele Norris. Washington, D.C.–based Editor Leah Latimer had extraordinary gifts for listening and coaching. Legendary Washington Post editor Ben Bradlee once vaunted Varner's story as the best in the paper on a particular day.

Truth Tellers: *The Power and Presence of Black Women Journalists Since 1960*

Bradlee's endorsement of her news story—about a boy conducting a social science experiment on the kiss-and-ride lane at a D.C. area Metro station—is as close to bragging as Varner seems to get. Even though she has been set apart at times in her career, including being twice nominated for journalism's golden crown, the Pulitzer Prize, Varner is more likely to put a spotlight on others. Varner is that kind of woman, journalist, and educator who lets her body of work speak for itself.

That list includes the Pulitzer nominations for co-authoring "Are We There Yet?," a 1998 series examining affirmative action in Washington State and several years later for commentary in the *Seattle Times* and a career at three of the best newspapers in the country: the *Washington Post*, the *Seattle Post-Intelligencer*, and the *Seattle Times*. Varner co-authored *Stories That Cover Us: Meditations and Fiber Art by the Pacific Northwest African American Quilters*, a book of luminous, evocative photographs and essays about Black women and quilt making She also had a stint at United Press International (UPI), where she covered former Washington Mayor Marion Barry's arrest on charges of cocaine possession and the subsequent fallout affecting the nation's capital and the nation. In the mid-1980s Varner joined Missouri Democratic Congressman Bill Clay, starting as an administrative assistant before working as a legislative aide and speechwriter. She later won a prestigious Knight Fellowship to study at Stanford University during the 2003-2004 academic year.

Varner graciously discusses her work, and her place in journalism, as an African American woman born, raised, and trained in a post–Civil Rights environment. When the triumvirate of modern civil rights history was being made—the 1963 March on Washington, passage of the Civil Rights Act in 1964, and of the Voting Rights Act of 1965—Varner was too young for kindergarten. Born abroad, her family moved in 1964 from Stuttgart, Germany, where her father was in the U.S. Army, to Seat Pleasant, in Prince George's County, Maryland. Today, Prince George's County, is one of the wealthiest African American communities in the country.

The shift from living in Europe to living in Washington, D.C., hit home for Varner when Martin Luther King, Jr. was assassinated in April

Lynne K. Varner

1968. Her family climbed the hill of their Seat Pleasant backyard and watched the smoke rise as the nation's capital convulsed and burned with anger. Varner had little direct experience with racial segregation but realizes now that her family and many other Black families were treated by whites with "fear and disdain" as they settled into suburban Washington communities. She also recalls being bused from her neighborhood elementary school to the mostly white Forestville, Maryland, where her mother became the first Black president of the North Forestville Elementary School PTA, a role her mother sought primarily, Varner believed, "to have some influence, some way of keeping her daughters and other Black students safe. She thought her presence could help calm the roiling waters."

Despite such protection and advocacy, Varner had to scrap and push to get to where she is today.

"Life," Varner said, "would have been a lot easier if I had the wind at my back. I've actually had the wind at my face."

After twenty-five years in journalism, Varner joined the leadership team at Washington State University in 2014 as associate vice president of public affairs in Seattle. In 2017, she was named associate vice chancellor, at the university's North Puget Sound campus in Everett. She oversees community engagement, student pathways, and marketing and communications that support student recruitment and retention, and is chief of staff to the chancellor of the Everett campus. In 2019, Varner became the chair of Cascade Public Media's Board of Directors, helping to clear the pathway for a new frontier media company that pairs for-profit and not-for-profit business models.

In all her leadership roles, Varner is in it for the work—the words and community—rather than an ability to flex power. She once told an interviewer: "Authority is the least thing that I need because I don't want to tell you what to do. I want to help you realize what you need to do and want to do it."

That attitude is at the heart of who Varner is and why she is successful.

Raised in wealthy Prince George's County, Maryland, Varner has always wanted to do something and be good at it. She started her first media company when she was 8: a newspaper, laid out on notebook paper, formatted in columns, with bylines and ads for dish detergent, and named for the city of St. Louis, where relatives lived. The news was real, albeit the stories were about animals, kids on bicycles, and other activities in her neighborhood.

"They were like the ones I had seen in a real newspaper. I was copying something that was impressing me at the moment," said Varner, whose own family had not yet acquired the status for which "PG County" would come to be known.

A voracious reader dubbed "Bookworm" by her siblings, Varner was an A student in English classes and loved to write. Yet, when it came time for her to prepare for college, she was left to fend for herself. She would be the first in her family to earn a college degree and at the beginning of that path, no teacher, guidance counselor, peer, or family member stepped up to guide her. She was encouraged to take shorthand, typing, and home economics in school in preparation for life as a secretary or someone's wife. Her parents had not attended college, and so they did not set that standard, in the late 1970s, for their fourth and most bookish child.

Whether writing or speaking, she weaves extemporaneous threads of strong, simple prose that tie listeners to the subject, the person, the memory that she is crafting. Here, it ties us to her parents' influence.

"We subscribed to the *Washington Post* and the *Evening Star*, because my father would come home from work and he had to read his paper—like things had changed that much during the day," Varner says, laughing. "My father and that military structure really helped. When I feel myself getting lazy, it doesn't feel good if I haven't accomplished anything. I always have to have something going on. That came from him.

"Seeing my mother walk out of the house every day with a suit on (was inspiring). You didn't have to wear a suit every day, but you did if you wanted to hobnob with white executives. She stood out because she was African American and at the senior level it was mostly white. She went to work every day no matter how tired she was from taking care of five kids. That taught me about looking the part even if you don't feel it. She worked for the federal Department of Housing and Urban Development for nearly forty-five years, which is how a Black woman without a college degree was able to climb. She had the intellect, the grit and the experience to climb, instead of a resume full of degrees."

Varner, though, wanted more. A family disruption that caused her to be placed in foster care as a teenager, led to a mentor relationship with a social worker with a master's degree. Varner asked the meaning of the "MSW" after the woman's name. The answer—master of social work—led to a discussion that whetted Varner's taste for higher education.

"I knew that [college] existed, but I didn't think it existed for me," Varner said of being inspired to prepare for college. "In school, we students would create 'winners and losers' and 'most likely to succeed,' and we would lavish them with knowledge and success. And if you're not chosen, you have to fight to get on that on-ramp." Varner fought.

"I started with taking the SAT cold, at 8 a.m. on a Saturday with no preparation. I just sat down and said, 'You are intelligent. Let's do this.'"

As a student, Varner entered the University of Maryland in the fall after high school graduation. Choosing journalism as her major, she flowed with every experience she could tap, writing for two campus newspapers and hosting a Sunday morning gospel show on campus radio. She also landed a job writing travel pieces for the trade publication *Candy Wholesaler Magazine*.

"I never go into anything halfway," said Varner, who ultimately graduated from the University of Maryland's Global Campus.

Her first post-college job was a five-year stint on Capitol Hill with Clay, the Missouri congressman, during the Reagan administration. In

Truth Tellers: *The Power and Presence of Black Women Journalists Since 1960*

1988, Varner got the job at UPI in Washington, D.C., where she worked six months without a byline but hoarded valuable lessons on writing and reporting by handling called-in copy from the likes of Helen Thomas, the vaunted wire service reporter who was known for asking hard-edged questions from her front-row seat among the White House Press Corps.

"I loved listening to reporters dictate these stories to me by phone, from city council meetings and foreign desks and the White House," Varner said. "Helen Thomas was on Air Force One a lot. It was really impressive to hear these brilliant writers out there in the field giving you fully formed sentences, practically writing the story as they spoke."

As much as she learned about writing and style at UPI, Varner landed the job there because of networking: meeting someone on the UPI foreign desk and confiding that she'd always wanted to be a journalist. One day he asked for her resume and passed it on. Varner stayed at the now defunct news service job for two and a half years, working her way up to general assignment on the Metro desk, covering everything that moved. The Marion Barry story broke on one of her shifts.

"I hightailed it to the Vista Hotel and the mayor was still there upstairs and I was among some of the first reporters on the scene and, I was able to dictate. I'm out in the field calling in pieces of the story, I stayed on that story the whole night" and for the next several weeks. And that, she adds is "how I got to the *Washington Post*."

Varner went to the *Post* with a resume full of clips about Marion Barry and other stories, such as the drug trafficking trial of Rayful Edmonds, a drug kinpin who once led D.C.'s biggest crack-smuggling ring in a large family-run organization. She wanted to cover Barry's trial at both UPI, and now at the *Post*, although she didn't get the opportunity to do so at either organization. Instead, at the *Post*, she was assigned to one of its bureaus covering Prince George's County—"the county I grew up in and knew like the back of my hand."

"I did not even ask for a bigger salary," Varner said. "This opportunity to be among some of the best journalists in the world, to be guided by some of the best editors in the world, I thought that was going to be way more valuable to me than what you pay me.

"I knew I was living my dream. I didn't feel like 'You're not paying me a lot,' which they weren't. I didn't feel like 'Oh, you stuck me in a bureau,' which they did. I just thought, 'Oh, I'm so glad to be here and have this opportunity to learn from the best.'" Which she did.

There came a time in 1992, that Varner again wanted more. After three years, she wanted in—to be downtown in the main newsroom. She talked to Milton Coleman, a senior editor, who eventually would go on to become deputy managing editor at the *Post*. Coleman was African American and known for guiding many of the minority journalists at the paper. Varner went to him expecting a gateway into the main newsroom but instead was presented a buzzer. Coleman told her he couldn't promise anything would happen soon, that there was a "deep ditch" of other talented writers all wanting more. The two continued the discussion, and it ended with Coleman's advice: "Sometimes you gotta leave to make people love you." Varner worked through her initial disappointment and then called the *Seattle Post-Intelligencer*. Once she said her name and told them where she worked, her call was put directly through to the city editor. No waiting. "I said, 'I would like to speak to the metro editor' and nobody said, 'Who do you think you are?'" recalled Varner. "They all said, 'Hold on.'"

Varner began with a familiar beat, education reporting. In 1995, she moved to the *Seattle Times*—twelve years before the *Post-Intelligencer* published its final print edition and became an online-only newspaper—moving from reporter to the editorial board and opinion page columnist.

"I stayed at the *Times* for nineteen years. The reason why I stayed is because what I wanted at the [*Washington*] *Post* I was able to get from the *Times*," Varner said. "The more that I asked for, the more they gave me, all the way up to joining the editorial board and having a column."

Sometimes you gotta leave to make people love you.

Her Pulitzer contenders were for a series with a reporting partner on affirmative action, titled "Are We There Yet?" and another about a challenge to Seattle's desegregation policy before the U.S. Supreme Court.

Among her personal best is an outrage column in the wake of Trayvon Martin's shooting death. The African American teen from Florida was slain at the hands of a neighborhood-watch vigilante, who targeted Martin in February 2012 as he walked at night from a convenience store, through a gated neighborhood, back to the townhouse of his father's girlfriend. Varner, the mother of a now 20-year-old African American son, was incensed at the "murder."

"It was not the first time that someone had criminalized a harmless activity of a young Black man," Varner said. "It really hit me hard. It was the first time that I could have seen that being my son. So, I wrote a couple of fiery pieces about it.

"I recall feeling like a mama bear, who, upon witnessing the killing of her cub, sets out to destroy everything in her path. My claws were my words, and my path was the opinion-page.

"I was full of rage and to me rage is meaningless if you don't drive it to something."

Another favorite was the story she wrote after returning from her Knight Fellowship at Stanford, where columnists had been encouraged to write to show who they were. Varner wrote about the foster care system and that she had, for a time, been one of its wards.

Her parents were divorcing when she, a younger brother, and an older sister were placed in other custodial care, where Varner stayed until she entered college at 18. Varner now has good relations with her parents—Henry Varner and Julia Clark—both of whom went on to marry other people and are now in their nineties.

She credits their influence for what she has achieved. Her veteran father always insisted that the family was up, bathed, and dressed early in the morning, no matter the day. After his military service, he worked a variety of jobs, including for a dairy company and the Virginia penal system. Julia Clark, who during the family's time in Germany had worked retail, was a stylish woman who climbed her way up to middle management in the U.S. Department of Housing and Urban Development (HUD). She retired from HUD after more than forty years, with a title seemingly as long as the wall of plaques honoring her achievements that stretched down a long corridor of her third-floor suburban Maryland home.

"They didn't go to college and didn't set that expectation, so I was the first one to earn a college degree," Varner says. "But they did say go out and work hard and make a life, own a house, and keep our family safe."

She has exceeded her parents' expectations, although not their particular paths. While successful in her East Coast Washington enclave, Varner's life was illuminated after moving to the West Coast, where she met her husband, had her son, and put down powerful journalistic roots. She's rubbed elbows with some of journalism's greats and ruffled the feathers of those affected by journalism's mandates, yet seems to have never lost the common touch. As generous as she is about other journalists, even as she explains their gifts, Varner's own resume, filled with achievement and eloquent storytelling is incomplete. There are still other projects, other frontiers to forage and other stories to be told.

"Partly because of the work I am doing with Cascade Public Media, where we've been able to build a solid financial model for journalism and better reflect the diverse communities we serve, I am full of optimism when I talk to aspiring journalists," said Varner. "I tell them to step up and into their place as the next generation of chroniclers holding this country and all within it accountable.

"It won't be easy," she added. "Journalism has many detractors. Money is still tight. But I have always been guided by one of my favorite spirituals, 'Ain't Gonna Let Nobody Turn Me Around.' This is a different day with different challenges but our refrain should be the same, 'we're not going to let anyone turn us around.'"

Cathy Gant Hill is a freelance editor, writer, and educator who worked fourteen years as a reporter covering arts, county government, and consumer affairs for the Greensboro (NC) News & Record. She lives in Greensboro, North Carolina.

Chapter 7

Sheila Robinson Solomon

When Patience Becomes the Best Equalizer—Providing Relief and Solace Becomes Her Legacy

Sheila Robinson Solomon knew little about medicine as a youngster but recalls feeling a sense of ease every time Dr. Russell E. Reid, whose office was within walking distance of her home, made house calls to examine her grandmother in their Newport News, Virginia, neighborhood.

Solomon appreciated Reid's soothing nature, a trait other doctors rarely exhibited to her grandmother, who left her home in rural Virginia to spend winters with her daughter and other family members.

"I don't know that it was medicine as much as what I saw in Dr. Reid and his bedside manner," Solomon said. "And I thought, *That is what I could do.*"

With Reid's assistance, Solomon's desire to become a physician led to an internship at Newport News's Whittaker Memorial Hospital during her senior year in high school. Then she realized that comforting others also involved blood, body fluids, and test tubes. Becoming a doctor no longer appealed to her.

Yet the desire to help others stayed with Solomon throughout her life and career in journalism, which included stints at *Newsday* (Long Island, NY), the *Daily Press* (Newport News, VA), the *Charlotte (NC) Observer*, and *Chicago Tribune*.

Solomon arrived at the *Chicago Tribune* in 2002, nearly thirty years after her first full-time job in journalism. It was a pivotal moment for her, although she never sought to be in management. The *Tribune* was then Chicago's largest newspaper with a circulation of more than one million on Sundays and a daily circulation of 689,026. Solomon joined the *Tribune* as the senior editor for recruitment and led staff development. After seven years, she become the *Tribune*'s cross media editor, charged with coordinating resources among the Chicago Media Group newsrooms.

"I've always believed that change comes faster if you're inside," referring to her longtime affiliation with the Tribune Company and, in Charlotte, Knight Ridder, which formerly owned the *Charlotte Observer*. "There's something about me that allows me not to come home angry if I didn't get a position." Her voice is smooth and soothing like that of a favorite evening radio host. It's difficult to imagine her raising her voice or expressing anger.

"Some didn't believe that if they waited their turn would come," she said, alluding to impatient younger reporters disenchanted about promotions denied or pay disparities compared to their white counterparts. "I can be patient. So, for a total of thirty-eight years when the supervision came, it was my turn."

Getting closer to the top for Solomon not only meant having patience and perseverance. It sometimes involved fighting feelings of loneliness and invisibility.

Solomon remembers such experiences mostly during high school when she rode the bus to a majority white high school rather than walk four blocks to attend Hampton's all-Black high school. This was the late 1960s and Virginia, like other Southern states, was immersed in desegregation and school choice.

"As a Black student, there was no way not to stand out, not to sometimes be 'the only,' not to feel 'othered' by white peers. At the same time, it was a temporary state of mind because, at the end of the day, I always returned to my family and neighbors where I didn't stand out for being Black and where I knew people expected I'd always be there."

Along with her parents, Ernest L. Robinson and Fannie Celeste Gillis Robinson, her high school teacher, Jill Cutler, also helped her feel less isolated. Cutler, was a friendly woman in her twenties and much younger than other teachers in the school.

"Maybe she was just a darn good teacher, a good person, and empathizing with her students—even ones like me who didn't look like her—was innate. So I've never forgotten what it's like to be the only or to feel like the only. Being there for someone, even a stranger, was never a big reach for me when a new person walked into a room."

Still toying with the idea of becoming a doctor when she became a student at Hampton University in 1970, Solomon changed her mind after discovering all the math and science classes necessary for medical school. Because she was a good writer, she turned to journalism, initially thinking that she would focus on radio reporting. During her junior year, she worked for the weekly *Hampton (VA) Monitor*. She later landed an internship at the *Daily Press* in Newport News.

"At that time, you wouldn't see many people of color at newspapers as reporters or as subjects," she said. "Jessie Rattley, who was the city's first Black mayor, couldn't get photos in the newspaper. There was picketing [to change that]."

It was perhaps then that Solomon, with her calm, quiet demeanor, constructed a road map for her life after college. The allure of all the things promised to young Black people after decades of discrimination, civil unrest, and social inequality beckoned those who bravely entered the growing professions of law, academia, and journalism. One professor in particular, George E. Cullen, Jr., who had worked for the *Daily Press*, encouraged her news writing abilities.

Solomon's professors ensured that their graduates were well versed in showing empathy to others and in knowing that they owed a debt to society. Many of her Black and white professors had left their own newsrooms to train Hampton's journalism students. The faculty maintained their newsroom connections, which meant that professional editors and producers routinely visited the historically Black university's campus.

"We were taught about the unselfishness you should be able to bring to any situation," she said, noting how Hampton University helped Howard University start its journalism program. Solomon saw her chance to enter this burgeoning world of news and information where she could make a difference in the lives of people who looked like her.

Adding to her excitement was what she saw while on a college class visit to the *Daily Press*'s gleaming new building. "I remember feeling awestruck, hearing the clacking of the keys when entering the building. I still have some of the materials that they gave us and remember seeing cold-type journalism. So I got the feeling, *this is something I should do*." Further fueling her thirst for news as a summer intern was interviewing entertainers, such as B. B. King and Stevie Wonder, during the city's annual Hampton Jazz Festival.

"I think I was a bit starstruck, but it also taught me not to be starstruck."

Solomon's work for the *Monitor*, coupled with her internship at the *Daily Press*, resulted in five job offers by the time she graduated from Hampton in 1974. *Time* magazine and *Newsday* were interested in hiring her, as well as the *Daily Press*, the *Richmond Times-Dispatch*, and the *Providence Journal*.

"I remember sitting on a campus bench, facing the Hampton River with a recruiter from *Time*. *Time* wanted me to be a researcher and that

Truth Tellers: *The Power and Presence of Black Women Journalists Since 1960*

Sheila Solomon (standing) at her first full-time reporting job at Newsday in 1974. She is with editors Brian Williams and Mike Unger (sitting).

is why I turned them down. Who knows how things would've turned out. I ended up taking the job at *Newsday*. When I went to *Newsday* that was an era of where newspapers were trying to bring in African Americans."

Solomon worked for *Newsday* six months before returning to Hampton to get married. She was hired at the *Daily Press* as a copy editor. Her son, Linwood, was born and when he turned 3, she received a call from Al Johnson, an affable Black newsman who often recruited African Americans for the *Charlotte Observer*.

It was 1984 and by then Solomon was a divorced single mother. Johnson, promising her a job as a regional copy editor in Charlotte, convinced Solomon to join the *Charlotte Observer*.

"I bought into everything they told me they were going to do," said Solomon. "I don't remember how long I'd been at the paper when they said I'd be a production editor rather than a regional copy editor. I went to Al who literally got on his knees and said, 'Please forgive me, I did not know.'"

The job required her to work on weekends, and Solomon sometimes found it hard to get a babysitter for her son. That meant her son sometimes joined her at work. Although Solomon eventually became a member of the editorial board and the newspaper's letters editor, another setback occurred when she became seriously ill and needed surgery. She survived, and so did her job. The newspaper provided her with a computer to work from home until she was well enough to return to the office.

"When I was sick they did not cut my salary. People kept my son; some coworkers told me not to worry. When the doctor released me to return to the office, I went back to my regional copy editing position before moving to the editorial board," she said, adding that she worked on other desks, too, including serving as editor of *Straight Up*, a section for teens.

Meanwhile, Solomon's son was becoming a teenager.

Although she did not travel much when her son was younger, she eagerly agreed to do so when the newspapers' leaders asked her to attend the National Association of Black Journalists annual convention. This was around the time when large newsrooms started identifying editors and newsrooms to do recruiting. She was already ahead of the trend, frequently interviewing new newsroom prospects, many of them women.

Despite overtures from other newsrooms, Solomon decided to stay in Charlotte, largely because of the bond established among the African American news staff. They counted on one another to help ease the pain of working during holidays and to deal with issues involving hiring, promotions, and salaries. It was not unusual for her to hear stories about less-experienced and younger white journalists receiving promotions over seasoned Black journalists.

"They were just tired of it and weren't getting paid," Solomon said, and many of them began leaving.

As much as she regretted seeing her colleagues leave, Solomon was up for the job of traveling and recruiting people to work at the *Observer*. Similar to the women in Terry McMillan's novels, she was not only waiting to exhale but also ready to get her groove back.

Truth Tellers: *The Power and Presence of Black Women Journalists Since 1960*

"I was contemplating having fun. My son was about to go to high school," she said. "The recruiting was never a choice for me [in terms of saying yes]. I didn't want to miss out."

Despite the disappointments and setbacks often presented during her career—feeling overlooked or misled—Solomon never let them defeat or define her.

"Even with all that, I've always felt and still feel at home in newsrooms. I don't know why. I think it's where I belong."

Solomon was always honest with her colleagues. This practice continued when, after thirteen years in Charlotte, she returned to the *Daily Press* in Virginia in 1997 "in a position of high leadership and high recognition in a big office with sunlight." She was the newspaper's staff development and reader editor.

"It didn't change when I got to Chicago," she continued. "I had a glass office and once people got to know me, they became comfortable enough to come and talk to me. Also, I may have been the only African American in the position I had and I was reporting to the managing editor. People felt free to talk to me and I wasn't their editor. I would always ask their permission — *What do you want me to do?* — before speaking on their behalf."

Part of her job in Chicago was helping senior-level editors get to know their reporters and staffs because the windy city's news operation could swallow her previous newsrooms.

"I remember my first tour in the newsroom and there were 200 people in the features department. That was a lot more than we had in Charlotte."

So was the Tribune Tower where the newspaper was housed with its more than twenty floors with corporate offices outfitted with "beautiful fireplaces, humongous wooden desks, luscious thick carpeting, and views of Lake Michigan."

Solomon's courtship with the *Chicago Tribune* began in the late 1990s when she was at the *Daily Press,* by then a Tribune Company newspaper.

Anne Marie Lipinski, the *Tribune's* first woman editor, told Solomon that Sheila Wolfe, a *Tribune* recruiter, was retiring.

Solomon flew to Chicago with no intentions of working there, and the city's cold weather confirmed her thoughts. As it turned out, the job went to someone else. Another call came in 2002, and this time Solomon bit. Once again, her patience paid off, including a six-figure salary and bonuses.

Looking back on her career, Solomon who met Barack Obama, the first African American president, during a *Chicago Tribune* editorial board meeting ("He took my hand and held onto it.") has "lived the dream that so many of us as journalists have to be successful." While she is proud to have been part of the change in diversifying the nation's newsrooms, she admits that she never thought it would take so long.

"I thought that in the seventies when all of these papers were looking for Black [journalists], I really felt that we would move up the ranks faster. I thought there would be more (people) wanting us to be in the newsroom.

When the Tribune announced in 2011 that Solomon was being laid off, it was such a somber time that Solomon called her sister to ask, *What am I doing?*

Colleagues were in shock over her forced retirement. "Men cried. Women cried." Solomon consoled her colleagues and let them know it would be OK. Then 63, Solomon already had plans for her second act: to volunteer to campaign for the man who had held on to her hand three years before—President Barack Obama who was seeking reelection in 2012.

"I just wanted to do a lot of different things. I was curious about being a pollster and registering voters, and hiring people."

After the campaign in which she served as a call center volunteer at the Obama For America National Headquarters in Chicago, Solomon taught as an adjunct professor at Columbia College in Chicago and was a contract recruiter for Journatic News Service. In 2013, she joined the multimedia production company Rivet360 and is now the strategic alliance manager.

When speaking with young people today about their career choices, Solomon speaks honestly.

"I try to tell them [that] if this is a profession you chose because of an insatiable curiosity about things and people you know nothing about, if you know your job and you know what the people supervising you have entrusted you with, and [if] you're feeling good about it and they're feeling good about it, you stick with that and let it take you where it takes you."

Chapter 8

Wanda Lloyd

Pushing Back, Moving Forward—Education and Tenacity
Led to Journalism's Pinnacle

Wanda Lloyd's 2020 autobiography, *Coming Full Circle: From Jim Crow to Journalism*, begins in her segregated hometown of Savannah, Georgia, and doesn't end after she lands executive level roles at one of the leading American newspapers, *USA Today*. Stops at the *Providence (RI) Evening Bulletin*, the *Miami Herald*, the *Atlanta Journal*, and the *Washington Post* were launching pads for her position at *USA Today* and later as a managing editor for the *Greenville (SC) News* and executive editor at the *Montgomery (AL) Advertiser*.

When Lloyd left the newspaper business in 2013, nearly ten years after joining the *Montgomery Advertiser* in 2004, she returned home to work at Savannah State University as chair of the Department of Journalism and Mass Communications.

In *Coming Full Circle*, Lloyd describes a life in which she was primed for success by her close-knit home and community— her village, she calls it in the memoir. Surrounded by a family of educated women, including her grandmother, Oper Lee Walker, who, along with Lloyd's aunt, Catherine Walker Williams, raised her, it was expected that Lloyd would follow the family tradition of attending and graduating from Spelman College, the private, elite college for Black women in Atlanta. Lloyd's mother, Gloria Walker, was a busy career woman, forging her own path, eventually becoming an executive buyer for the Army and Air Force Exchange Service. When Lloyd was born, her mother was nineteen years old and soon to be divorced from Lloyd's father, John Henry Smalls. Except for when she was a baby, Lloyd saw her father again once when she was a student at Spelman College, she writes in her book. Thus, raising Gloria's daughter was shared by other family members.

Growing up, Lloyd's grandmother often schooled her granddaughter about how Black people had to navigate dealing with white folks during the 1950s and 1960s, an era when Jim Crow segregation laws ruled. The lessons would serve her well in college and beyond.

"When we go downtown you have to look your best," she would tell me, Lloyd writes in her book. "We don't want the white folks to think the Walkers don't know how to carry ourselves."

Lloyd was constantly reminded that "as a colored woman" she would always have to "be better, make good grades, look better, jump higher, wear better looking clothes . . ."

"Bring attention to yourself for good reasons," her grandmother told her.

Joining her Alfred Ely Beach High School newspaper, the *Beach Beacon*, was Lloyd's first step toward her newspaper career. Ella P. Law, her journalism teacher, noticed Lloyd's creative story ideas, her writing and storytelling abilities, and her willingness to help students with their assignments.

As with many fledgling student journalists, Lloyd was excited by newswriting, enjoyed seeing her name in print, and was gratified by the positive feedback she received from fellow students and her teachers. She was ecstatic when Law appointed her to be the *Beach Beacon*'s editor-in-chief in her senior year.

Lloyd's introduction to the Dow Jones Newspaper Fund coincided with her new title. Paul Swenson, the Newspaper Fund's executive director, proposed a trial program at Savannah State College (now Savannah State University) for African American teachers and some of their students. Lloyd was among six students in the 1964 program studying newswriting, interviewing, newspaper design, and photography.

"We gained skills for news judgment, how to motivate staff to recognize a good story when they hear about it, how to raise money to support our journalism, and how to avoid getting into trouble with school administrators who universally had more appreciation for censoring the news than for First Amendment freedom of the press," Lloyd said in *Coming Full Circle*.

Lloyd continued to expand her journalism portfolio by becoming the first Black reporter for *Teen Times*, a tabloid section in the *Savannah Evening Press*. Her stories included school fashion trends and co-ed woodworking classes.

After graduating from high school in 1967, Lloyd enrolled at Spelman College where she majored in English and continued to pursue journalism by taking courses at nearby Clark College (later Clark Atlanta University) because Spelman did not have a journalism program. She wrote for the *Spelman Spotlight* and she later became editor of her college newspaper. At the end of her junior year, Lloyd received a three-week Newspaper Fund fellowship at Temple University in Philadelphia and an internship in Providence, Rhode Island, in 1970, which was the first year African Americans were included in the internship program.

"I felt like we were really well-prepared from a technical and professional standpoint," said Lloyd. "We learned copy editing, rules of the composing room, and terminology about typography."

At the end of the program at Temple, Lloyd was dispatched to the *Providence Evening Bulletin* for her summer copy editing internship. "I was told that there had never been a Black newsroom professional at the newspaper," said Lloyd. "Until then, I'd had limited interaction with white people. When I went to Temple, that was the first time I'd ever been around white people consistently. There was one other Black girl in the program."

Just before her graduation from Spelman in 1971, an occasion in which her grandmother attended in a wheelchair two months before her death, Lloyd called the *Providence Evening Bulletin* to let them know she was ready to return to work there. She decided to return to Providence when her efforts to secure a copyediting position at one of the Cox-owned newspapers in Atlanta proved fruitless. Atlanta's daily newspaper was hiring Blacks as reporters so that the Black community could see that it employed Black journalists, she was told. The paper would not hire her to work the copy desk because copy editors worked inside the building and were not visible to Black readers.

After a year at the *Evening Bulletin*, she received a call from Jack White, a reporter for *Time* magazine, who was calling on behalf of journalist Robert C. Maynard. White said Maynard was about to direct the Summer Program for Minority Journalists at Columbia University and wanted her to be a copy editor for the program, she writes in *Coming Full Circle*. Lloyd's editors in Providence approved her leave-of-absence request to work with the program, and off she went to New York to join "a star-studded faculty" that included Maynard, Charlayne Hunter-Gault and Earl Caldwell. The program trained second- career or non-traditional students who produced *Deadline*, a weekly laboratory newspaper.

"Each week we went about building a story budget for the eight-page tabloid newspaper with stories by our student participants who covered live news in New York City and on the Columbia campus."

The move to Providence proved pivotal in other ways. In addition to working on the national, international and state news copy desks, editing copy, writing headlines and designing pages, she met her future husband,

Willie Lloyd, who was stationed nearby in the U.S. Navy. The couple dated for several weeks but lost touch when he was deployed to Diego Garcia, an Island in the Indian Ocean, and later when she moved for a job at the *Miami Herald* in 1973. In Miami, like in Providence where she worked on various copy desks, she enjoyed the newsroom's environment and its diverse staff of reporters and copy editors. She formed lasting friendships with several Black colleagues.

Yet, when she realized she still had a desire to work at one of the newspapers in Atlanta, Lloyd flew to the city one Saturday morning to meet the managing editor, whose name she did not learn until she arrived at the newspaper's security desk. She met the editor, told him about her work experience, and asked for a job on the copy desk. Informed that there were no openings, she returned to Miami the same day. Within weeks, she received a call to work for the *Atlanta Journal* and joined the newspaper in 1974, eighteen months after she joined the *Miami Herald*.

Lloyd soon realized that she had made a grave mistake. She was assigned to the universal copy desk where "shoveling" copy was customary, a dire consequence of not doing her homework before she was hired.

"We weren't selecting photos; it was mostly copyediting and mostly wire [not local] copy," she said.

Fate intervened along with Lloyd's former friend, Willie Lloyd. Wanda Lloyd called Elsie Carper, a *Washington Post* newsroom recruiter who had encouraged her to try out at the *Washington Post* in the past. When Willie Lloyd tracked down Wanda Smalls (at the time) in Atlanta, they became engaged soon after. She traveled to Washington, D.C., for a tryout at the *Post*. Soon thereafter, Lloyd quit her job in Atlanta, moved to Virginia, and she received another call from Carper. In June 1975, Lloyd was hired as a production editor for the *Washington Post*. She was excited to work at the prestigious newspaper whose reputation had soared after its coverage of the 1972-1974 Watergate scandal, a burglary of Democratic Party headquarters in Washington involving President Richard Nixon and members of his administration. Ongoing reporting by the *Post* and other newspapers led Congress to approve articles of impeachment proceedings against Nixon for obstruction of justice, abuse of power, and contempt of Congress. Thus, Nixon resigned on August 9, 1974.

The *Washington Post*'s allure faded somewhat for Lloyd during her first couple of months, given her late-night, early-morning work hours. She worked only among white men in the production room, a job she described as "the last line of defense to edit copy on the lead pages ... the last to correct misspelled words, and the last able to add quick and necessary facts to a story or fix errors caught in the proofing process between editions."

She no longer wore dresses or skirts, only slacks, because she was constantly bending over pages to make corrections while surrounded by men. While many of the men in the production room were supportive and kind, Lloyd said there was an occasional "intentional" brush of her behind by some of the men, and frequently, disparaging remarks about women's bodies did not escape her.

After two months in the composing room, Lloyd requested a transfer to a copy desk job in the newsroom. There, on the Metro copy desk, she settled into a more familiar routine until a pressman's strike a few weeks later resulted in damage to the newspaper's presses.

Lloyd, at the time a part-time employee (who was working a full-time schedule), and some of the other employees ended up not working for several weeks until the strike was resolved. Fearing that she would not be called back to work, Lloyd thought about a career in interior design, something she thought might be an alternative career, and she signed up for a class at a local community college. She was called back to work the day before her first design class began.

"There was a fire and a foreman was critically injured," said Lloyd, and "some people were followed home and injured along the way. Because of the picket line at the front of the building, some of us were encouraged to go through the loading dock" in the back of the building. A few months later, on the day the strike ended, Lloyd was offered a position as a full-time editor of the *Los Angeles Times / Washington Post* News Service, a job she held for ten years. Yet, after a time as she outgrew that job, Lloyd wanted to be an editor of the federal page—it was new, it was open, and it covered issues for those who were working for the government, the main industry in Washington, D.C. She did not get the job or others that she applied for, including one as an editor in the *Post*'s Outlook (Sunday opinion) section. She was told that she did not have "enough experience, depth, or savvy" for the jobs she sought.

"An editor said that I had no future [at the *Post*] because I didn't have enough depth or experience, although I had worked at the *Providence Bulletin*, in Miami, in Atlanta and the *Post*. I kept being denied," said Lloyd.

Lloyd eventually heard about a new newspaper under development—*USA Today*, which, over time, became and remains the Gannett Company's flagship daily newspaper.

Ben Bradlee, the legendary journalist who was executive editor of the *Post* from 1965 to 1991, "ridiculed [USA Today] and said that no one cared about charts and graphics," essential elements of the new, vibrant-looking daily," said Lloyd. Other editors and reporters across the country voiced similar reactions.

But Lloyd, who was always interested in technology and design, was intrigued by the new publication and ready to forge a new path. While she admired and respected Bradlee, calling him a "brilliant editor who, while a little rough around the edges, spoke honestly and cared a lot about reporters and was a great judge of talent," he was not the type of person "you'd go in [his office] and chat up." Lloyd remembers one meeting in which she, Metro columnist Dorothy Gilliam, and assistant city editor Marcia Greene had met with Bradlee to discuss the newsroom's declining diversity as many African Americans were leaving the newspaper.

Some Black employees also were disillusioned that not much progress had been made since several African American reporters, known as the

Metro Seven, filed a discrimination lawsuit against the *Post* in 1972, "alleging that the newspaper was 'denying Black employees an equal opportunity with respect to job assignments, promotional opportunities, including promotions to management positions and other terms and conditions of employment,'" wrote Lloyd, attributing the information to a 2002 *NABJ Journal* article. The meeting with Bradlee ended with no promises of change and "no promises of making retention of people of color a priority."

Lloyd decided that any change in her career was up to her. She resisted a call from *USA Today* in 1982 when she was pregnant with her daughter, Shelby. But when her former *Miami Herald* managing editor Ron Martin at *USA Today* reached out to her a few years later, she was ready to join the new newspaper, *USA Today*, which, contrary to the established newspapers that initially ridiculed the colorful publication with its emphasis on shorter stories, splashy photos and infographics, was getting good reviews by readers.

Lloyd became deputy managing editor for *USA Today*'s cover stories. A year later, in order to further develop her management skills, Lloyd was encouraged to participate in the two-month Maynard Institute Management Training Center, a program at Northwestern University in Illinois. She initially hesitated because her daughter was only four years old at the time, but her husband convinced her to attend.

"In one evening he put together a support network to help take care of their daughter. Neighbors and his sister all stepped in to help."

The Northwestern program changed her life. "It was like going to the Harvard MBA program with spreadsheets, HR profiles, business case studies, and newspaper math and accounting," she said, decades later during a luncheon interview in Savannah, Georgia. "Although the program lacked much of a news component, it included lessons about distribution, circulation, budgeting, macroeconomics, and microeconomics.

"We learned the whole thing. When I got back to *USA Today*, Ron Martin, executive editor, drilled me on what I learned. He promoted me to managing editor for newsroom administration, which then had 430 people [resources, salaries, five budgets totaling $40 million]. I went to the Maynard [Institute] program in 1987 and I was promoted the day I returned.

Lloyd supervised a staff that included an accounting person, three department assistants, and all summer interns. She also managed the loaner program, which "borrowed" staff members from other Gannett newspapers for three-month periods. Her salary jumped dramatically during her time at *USA Today*.

In 1996, the Lloyds decided it was time to head back to the South, where they desired a better way of life to raise their daughter. Wanda Lloyd was hired as a managing editor of the *Greenville (SC) News* in charge of several of the news operations plus administering the newsroom's business functions. While there, she also spearheaded the project to redesign the aging newsroom's physical assets. In her book, Lloyd describes the newspaper's long-standing usage of criminal suspects' mug shots on the front page, mostly displaying young Black men who had been arrested. That changed under her leadership.

She invited a Greenville Police Department major to meet with the paper's news editors. He explained that the mug shots stereotyped Black men in Greenville as criminals. At the end of the meeting, Lloyd told the editors: "From now on, we will no longer run mug shots of any suspects or arrested people on page one. Their race does not matter. Not white people or Black people, not men or women."

She loved Greenville with its mild weather and nearby mountain scenery, but a call to change came after living in the city for a few years. In 2000, she was asked to head up a new diversity initiative in Nashville, as executive director at what would become the Freedom Forum Diversity Institute at Vanderbilt University. The program was designed to provide journalism training to midcareer people of color who wanted to start second careers. Students ranged in age from their late twenties to sixties.

"My charge was to get the program off the ground while the building was being built," she said. "I would help design the interior of the new

32,000-square-foot, $7 million facility next door to the Freedom Forum's First Amendment Center."

Although initially hesitant to take the job because of her family's love for Greenville, Lloyd began her new role in Nashville in January 2001. She enjoyed the four-year experience, calling it the best job of her career. The program was successful in training dozens of journalists, but Lloyd found it difficult to get newsrooms to buy into the program by identifying and holding job slots for the newly trained journalists. Back then—and now—many news organizations were facing severe budget cuts and industry shifts. They found it difficult to hold open vacant positions for the Diversity Institute's graduates. Lloyd also was shaken by a 2003 Freedom Forum task force report that envisioned what the Diversity Institute might look like in 2012. It stated that the institute would be viable with the financial support of the newspaper industry.

Knowing that industry financial support would never happen, Lloyd decided to return home to Gannett, owner of *USA Today* and the *Greenville News*. Demonstrating the adroitness, confidence, and expertise she had acquired after decades of navigating newspapers, prestigious journalism organizations such as the American Society of Newspaper Editors, Associated Press Managing Editors, National Association of Minority Media Executives, the National Association of Black Journalists, and universities, along with watchful and sometimes wary communities, Lloyd called Phil Currie, Gannett's senior vice president for news. She asked whether a leadership position was available in the South. She asked about the newspaper in Montgomery, Alabama, to be exact.

In June 2004, Lloyd became executive editor of the *Montgomery Advertiser*, the first African American woman to hold that position. The experience was good, but she regrets the several rounds of layoffs, which involved some of the longer-term staff members who were forced out of their jobs and who lost benefits like their health insurance.

Gannett featured Wanda Lloyd in its 1993 annual report about her efforts to diversify the nation's newsrooms.

"It was disturbing to let go of that great talent, but the company was not making enough money," she said. "My memory is that shareholders wanted bigger profit margins. Technology, the economy, and a change in habits were to blame. Newspapers were losing readers and trust, and advertising revenue was declining. Circulation numbers and advertising go hand in hand. As editor, I had to deliver the news to employees who were about to be laid off; it had to be done immediately so that HR could cut off access to the building and computers. I was always given a number [dollar figures], and I had to figure out what was best for the paper."

Amid all the drama in Montgomery, some highlights included coverage of the fiftieth anniversary of the Montgomery Bus Boycott, the December 1, 1955, protest against the bus system in Alabama by civil rights activists and supporters until the U.S. Supreme Court upheld a district court ruling (*Browder v. Gayle*) that declared segregated bus laws as unconstitutional.

Lloyd retired from the *Advertiser* and daily journalism in 2013, but soon was being sought for another job that signaled the arrival of her full-circle career and life. She was invited to chair the mass communications program at Savannah State University, the same place she received her first formal introduction to journalism, thanks to her high school journalism teacher, Ella Law.

Wanda Lloyd as executive editor of the Montgomery Advertiser.

After spending three years at Savannah State, Lloyd left to focus on writing her book and other projects. Shortly after the publication of *Coming Full Circle*, she co-edited another book with her friend, novelist Tina McElroy Ansa, who had been her Spelman College freshman-year roommate. They published the collective of essays, *Meeting at the Table: African-American Women Write on Race, Culture and Community* shortly after the tragic death of George Floyd in Minneapolis. These two books followed another book project she co-edited in 2009, and *The Edge of Change: Women in the Twenty-First Century Press*.

Lloyd's career honors are many and include the Robert G. McGruder Award for Media Diversity, the Ida B. Wells Award for Media Diversity, and the Columbia University Career Achievement Award. She was inducted into the National Association of Black Journalists Hall of Fame in 2019.

She is a former director of the American Society of Newspaper Editors, a co-founder and chair of the National Association of Minority Media Executives, and she served as a member of the Dow Jones Newspaper Fund Board of Directors. Lloyd also served for twelve years on the journalism advisory boards of the Accrediting Committee of the Accrediting Council on Education for Journalism and Mass Communications.

Out of all of her career opportunities, Lloyd is most proud of her work with the Freedom Forum Diversity Institute and the hundreds of "children"—young journalists and others she has mentored.

Chapter 9

Patrice Gaines

Laughing in the Dark—In Advocating for the "Underdog,"
She Advocates for Everyone

Complex, gripping, and packed with details of life's seedy and unsavory vagaries are hallmarks of the storytelling produced by Patrice Gaines during her award-winning career as a *Washington Post* reporter. Over a span of sixteen years at the *Post*, many of Gaines's stories focused on society's so-called underdogs—mostly Black and brown people involved in gun or gang violence or young drug dealers gunned down in drive-by shootings.

Gaines, who joined the *Washington Post* in 1985, said she gravitated toward such stories, particularly those involving African American youth, because many of their trouble-filled lives resembled her own past.

Truth Tellers: *The Power and Presence of Black Women Journalists Since 1960*

She grew up as the eldest of seven children in a military family that lived in New Bern, North Carolina, where she was born, before moving to Quantico, Virginia; Beaufort, South Carolina; Washington, D.C.; and Lanham, Maryland. Her father, William Baxter Gaines, was a stern Marine and her mother, Eleanor Murrell Gaines, a housewife. She lacked a clear career path during her senior year in high school, and her plans to pursue commercial art had derailed by the time she graduated from Lanham's DuVal High School in 1967.

"By my last year in high school, I skipped classes, hooked school, came in hours after curfew and disobeyed my parents regularly, mainly to see [my boyfriend] Ben," Gaines wrote in her book *Laughing in the Dark: From Colored Girl to Woman of Color—A Journey from Prison to Power*.

At 19, Gaines was engaged and pregnant and living in Charlotte where her child's father introduced her to drugs. She became a user who saw herself as "more addicted to the guy than the drugs." Gaines said her drug use was about trying to find a way to relieve the pain she felt.

"I hated myself. In this country, I thought being Black—I was nothing," she confessed on a *Dateline* segment in the 1990s. "I thought being a woman—I was nothing. And I just thought personally—I was nothing."

Many of those days were filled with sexual abuse and depression, said Gaines, who was arrested with her boyfriend, Ben, in Charlotte at age 21 during a Steppenwolf concert. "I was charged with possession of heroin with intent to distribute and possession of a needle and syringe; both charges are felonies," she said, noting that, back then, she shot up heroin several times a week. She was held on a $100,000 bond and spent the next three weeks in jail before pleading guilty and being given a five-year probation.

Her daughter, Andrea, was 2 years old at the time—too young to be allowed in for visits. That experience, watching from the window as family held her daughter for her to see, but being unable to touch her or reassure her, was a turning point. Gaines eventually overcame her early struggles and three failed marriages to become a prize-winning *Washington Post* reporter, a writer for magazines such as *Essence* and *Black Enterprise*, and a notable author of two books. (At the time of this interview in 2015, Gaines was married for the fourth time. She has since divorced her fourth husband.)

"I was just feeling bad about myself," Gaines said of her earlier missteps. "Going to jail was a wake-up call. I went to community college and became a secretary. By that time, I started writing."

Her secretarial job was at the *Charlotte News*, and her writing began to make her feel better about herself. A professor, "Ms. Jones," at Johnson C. Smith University, even published some of Gaines's poetry in a literary review.

"I showed it [her poetry] to some of the other people in the newsroom. A circulation manager asked me to write for the employee newsletter. This was 1976," Gaines recalled. The following year she began working as a consumer columnist and research writer for the newspaper.

"Getting into the newsroom and seeing all the writers demystified the job," Gaines said. "I knew I wanted to write, but I didn't know how people made a living writing."

A friend mentioned the Maynard Institute Summer Program for Minority Journalists at the University of California, Berkeley, and Gaines quickly applied.

"When I was accepted, that's when I knew it was serious," she said. "This was for me like, 'Wow. Okay, I can do something with my life.'"

For Gaines, the program was a much-needed lifeline. She met fellow journalists Karen Howze and Jacqueline Trescott during the program. Howze developed a reputable career as a reporter and editor with newspapers in San Francisco, Long Island and Rochester, New York, Detroit, and Washington, D.C. In 1981, she was one of eight founding editors of *USA Today*. After leaving journalism, she used her law degree to advocate for children and people with disabilities, adoptions and the protection of the elderly, and later was a judge on the District of Columbia's Superior Court.

Trescott was already working at the *Washington Post* when Gaines met her, said Gaines. Over the years, Trescott's name became familiar to many

Truth Tellers: *The Power and Presence of Black Women Journalists Since 1960*

Washingtonians as well as readers throughout the country. She wrote for the *Washington Star* from 1970 to 1975, before moving to the *Washington Post*, where she was a cultural news reporter for the *Washington Post's* Style section for 37 years, according to her LinkedIn profile.

"We were eighteen people being trained to be journalists," said Gaines. "My first [reporting] job was at the *Miami News*. I was the third Black reporter to work there. I had no knowledge of journalism prior to that. The opportunity came to learn how to do it."

The summer program was more than enlightening, she recalled.

"I learned about [Robert] Bob Maynard, (the pioneering journalist for whom the program was named), and Earl Caldwell," she added. Caldwell, today a writer-in-residence at Hampton University, rose to fame as a reporter at *The New York Times* when he refused to disclose information to the FBI and the Nixon Administration involving his sources in the Black Panther party. The case, United States v. Caldwell, reached the U.S. Supreme Court in 1972 when the court ruled against him. The "Caldwell Case" led to the enactment of shield laws in many states that allow reporters to protect sources and information. Caldwell also was the only reporter present when the Rev. Dr. Martin Luther King, Jr. was assassinated.

Like many young Black journalists entering the newspaper industry in the 1970s, some of Gaines's relatives were unsure what her job entailed.

"My father thought I was going to be on television," she said, adding that he preferred that she would "get a good government job."

But adjusting to life in Miami was not easy as Gaines later wrote about in her 1994 autobiography, *Laughing in the Dark*.

"There were riots and Black people suddenly saw me as the enemy. I questioned myself a lot. Miami itself, despite the arrival of Haitians and Cubans, is very much the South and racist. I stayed there two grueling years. I had to buy a house because no one would rent to me."

Upon leaving Miami, Gaines moved to Washington, D.C. to help take care of her grandmother, who had suffered a stroke. After working temporary jobs for a while, she eventually was hired by the *Washington*

Star to cover education in Montgomery County, Maryland. Although Gaines didn't enjoy the job or being in the suburbs, she made the best of it by writing solid stories.

"Nobody knew the history of Blacks in those communities," Gaines said, intensity filling her voice during a 2015 interview in Charlotte, North Carolina, about twenty miles from her current South Carolina home. "We heard it on the radio and that was it."

Gaines worked for the *Star* until 1981, when the 129-year-old paper ceased publication.

Past feelings and doubts resurfaced. "I remember feeling after the *Star* closed, 'There I was without a job again.'"

Faced with finding a new job, Gaines decided that sharpening her writing skills was the best way to advance her journalism career. She enrolled at the University of the District Columbia and took English classes under the late novelist Gloria Naylor, author of such books as *The Women of Brewster Place*, *Linden Hills*, and *Mama Day*.

"A lot of good things were happening to the writing," Gaines said of her work during that time. "I focused on developing my writing outside of journalism."

Armed with a greater sense of confidence and strong writing samples, Gaines applied to the *Washington Post*.

"As it happens, there were some Black people who wanted me to work there, such as Milton Coleman and Vivian Aplin-Brownlee. She [Aplin-Brownlee] hired me to do freelance writing in 1983."

Gaines's unflinching approach to telling gut-wrenching stories about suicide attempts and other crime-laced human dramas impressed her editors. Yet, she did not impress them enough to warrant a pay raise.

"I was hired at the *Post* in 1985, and a local magazine published an article, about the disparity in pay among Black and whites and men and women," she said, adding that the article noted that she was the newspaper's lowest-paid reporter in 1986-87. "This was the heyday in Washington journalism circles, but Blacks were not paid as much. I remember having a conversation with Donald Graham, and they decided to put me on the quote 'fast track' because they were embarrassed about the article and because Black women were organizing and the union was helping us fight for better wages. They were being pressured."

Graham, who held several positions at the *Post*, including publisher and chairman of the board, was the son of Phillip L. and Katharine Meyer Graham. His father was publisher of the *Washington Post* from 1946 until 1961 and president of the Washington Post Company from 1947 until his death in 1963. His mother, Katharine Graham, served in several executive positions from 1963 until her death in 2001. Eugene Meyer, Graham's grandfather, purchased the *Washington Post* at a bankruptcy sale in 1933.

In hindsight, Gaines said her hesitancy to initially fight for more money was mainly attributed to her youth rather than a lack of confidence.

"I was a scared kid," Gaines said. "I should have said, 'You better give me my damn money!'"

While Gaines's background involving drugs was not a factor in how she thus far had been treated at the paper—she had concealed that part of her past—it was about to have an effect. She said she was forced to reveal her criminal record after she became part of a group of reporters involved in a legal cased filed against the paper.

"Our lawyers advised me to tell the paper before the court appearance so that it would not come out in court," she recalled.

After divulging the truth, she had to wait three months to be told by executive editor Ben Bradlee that she would be allowed to stay because "she was so damn talented."

Once her secret was out, Gaines was relieved. "I felt free that I'd never have to lie again. That alone freed me to be able to speak freely about it."

As a general assignment reporter on the city desk, Gaines said it was Ben Bradlee who assigned her the tag of writing about the "underdogs."

While some editors were uncomfortable with the way her stories "pushed readers' comfort zones," Gaines said, *Post* staffers such as Jackie Jones were supportive of her work.

"Jackie Jones was my editor at one point and she said she 'put on armor to fight for me daily.' She really did fight for my stories, which illustrates the importance of having Black people in positions where they can make these important decisions such as pitching and defending stories."

(In 2021, Jones became dean of the Morgan State University School of Global Journalism and Communication.)

After working on a murder case involving a 48-year-old Black woman, Catherine Fuller, for nearly three years, Gaines left the *Post* in 2001. She turned over her work to the Innocence Project because she felt the evidence against the 8th and H street crew, arrested and convicted of killing Fuller, didn't add up.

The case was reopened in 2012, eventually being argued before the U.S. Supreme Court in 2017. While they lost the case in a 6-2 decision, Justices Ruth Bader Ginsburg and Elena Kagan dissented.

In a 2020 interview with South Carolina's CN2 News, Gaines shared her feelings about the death of Ginsburg that same year, and the experience of bringing a case all the way to the Supreme Court.

"I really felt such an emotional loss when she [Ginsburg] died. I just felt like somebody who stood for me and my beliefs, and the way I looked at the world and the compassion that I have for people—I felt like somebody who stood there for me is gone."

Gaines went on to say that after fighting the Fuller case for years, having two justices agree with her made her feel seen and understood.

The ability Gaines had to identify with the people she wrote about was something she also saw as an asset.

"What I ended up finding is that it gave me a good amount of empathy that a number of people I was working with at the *Post* at that time did not have," Gaines told interviewer Michael Eric Dyson during an interview on NPR affiliate station WEAA-FM, Baltimore. The audio file appears on her website.

This was an area where Gaines knew that her own past gave her a unique perspective. She was able to walk into stories with a better understanding of the complexities of life and the ability to imagine that the person before her was not necessarily the person they could be, or even would be ten years from now. This type of nonjudgmental understanding from Gaines helped people open up to her.

It also brought her professional recognition. While at the *Washington Post*, Gaines was awarded First Place Commentary from the National Association of Black Journalists for the article "Tough Boys and Trouble—Those Girls Waiting Outside D.C. Jail Remind Me of Myself." And in 2009, she received a Soros Justice Media Fellowship to write a series of articles about the impact of incarceration on the Black community.

In addition to her journalism work, Gaines has also devoted herself to being a justice advocate and abolitionist intent on promoting her belief that crime can be reduced without depending on the mass incarceration of human beings.

In 2004, she opened the Brown Angel Center along with her friend Gaile Dry-Burton. The nonprofit runs monthly workshops for imprisoned women in Charlotte, North Carolina.

The lessons she shares with the women, about confronting their past and finding a new self-definition that allows them to release the shame and guilt they carry from the mistakes they have made, are ones Gaines wrote about in her second book, 1997's *Moments of Grace: Meeting the Challenge to Change*.

Some of those same themes are also present in the 2021 publication *Say Their Names: How Black Lives Came to Matter in America*. The book was the idea of award-winning journalist Michael H. Cottman, who invited Gaines, along with journalists Curtis Bunn, Nick Charles, and Keith Hairston, to write it with him.

Dealing with racial inequality in America, and spurred into action after the murder of George Floyd, the co-authors discuss individual topics that are united by the goal of giving voices to the voiceless.

Gaines uses her own personal experiences to write about the issue of locking up Black lives and the effect incarceration has on the lives of those who are labeled felons.

Today, Gaines is divorced from her fourth husband. The child she gave birth to as a teenager went on to graduate from Spelman College. She has also learned to accept her past and love herself.

Looking back over her life, Gaines admits that her journalism career provided many benefits by placing her in different situations she overcame, which led to a sense of confidence and accomplishment.

"I feel I had the opportunity for things that could help me in life. Yet, it's hard to give advice to future generations. I was taken advantage of because I worked during a time when we wrote stories that could be resold over and over by our employers and we did not get a drop of the profits."

Still, despite the disappointments endured, Gaines cherishes the access her career gave her to others' lives.

"I got to witness, but not live through personally, tragedy or the height of joy. It shaped how I saw the world—spiritually, politically—just seeing human beings at their most vulnerable moments, something that most people will never be able to see," she said. "I hope the passion remains with young journalists and they realize what a gift it is to witness history and witness people in their most human state."

Chapter 10

Barbara Ciara

"Fall Down, Get Up, Don't Whine"—From Early Missteps to Broadcast Stardom

By Cathy M. Jackson

"Fall down, get up, don't whine."

Those words in her mother's voice have run on a continuous loop, echoing in Barbara Ciara's ears and buttressing her life's ambition and dreams for over fifty years. Her legacy is of her making, but her mother was the mastermind, the wind beneath her wings.

Yet no legacy is built in a day: Ciara's emanates from the decades she honed a broadcasting career out of a bigger-than-life determination indigenous to her personality, the countless stories she told to uplift those who did not have a voice to speak for themselves, the drive that took her from the Pittsburgh projects to homelessness in New York City, to a GED, to a university scholarship in Arizona, to a $2.10-an-hour job as a production assistant at KZAZ-TV in Tucson.

Her final stop was Norfolk, Virginia, where she began at WVEC-TV, Channel 13 (1981), then WAVY-TV, Channel 10 (1983), back to WVEC-TV (1989), and currently to WTKR-TV, Channel 3, where she earns a six-figure salary as the weekday evening anchor.

She began searching for better prospects outside of Arizona when General Manager Gene Adelstein downsized the KZAZ news staff. She received two offers and chose the morning cut-in anchor/reporter position at Norfolk's WVEC in 1981. The return to the East Coast, and to Norfolk with its "rich cultural blend of people of color," appealed to her.

Norfolk and its three major TV stations and NPR outlet, WHRO-TV, gave Ciara opportunities to make her mark in the industry. In 1997, she was named the managing editor of Local News on Cable (LNC), an innovative media convergence project between the *Virginian Pilot*, WVEC, and cable TV stations. She established LNC's twenty-four-hour news system and taught reporters how to work in both print and television formats. During the same time, Ciara was managing editor of a joint venture between WVEC and WHRO and co-hosted the group's newsmagazine *This Week in Hampton Roads*. She left WVEC to move to WTKR in 2000, but a noncompete clause in her WVEC contract meant she could not appear on air at WTKR for a year during which she worked off-air as a managing editor.

Ciara did not miss being on camera. The break gave her time to earn a bachelor's degree and graduate summa cum laude from Hampton University. She also taught as an adjunct professor at Hampton.

When Ciara arrived in Norfolk, she said that Diana Morgan at WAVY-TV was the sole Black female anchor, and there were no journalists of color anchoring the prestigious news slot at 6 p.m. and 11 p.m. She left WVEC when General Manager Tom Chisman told her "the Tidewater market 'was not ready for a Black anchor in prime time,'" she said.

"I was determined to make a liar of him and eventually prevailed by getting rehired by WVEC (after he was long gone) to the position of 6 p.m. and 11 p.m. anchor with Jim Kincaid."

For most of her career, Ciara made liars out of many people, succeeding in the face of long odds to earn the right to cover major stories: on the ground during a Haitian uprising, aboard the USS *Eisenhower*, one of the first naval carriers to sail from Norfolk after 9/11; presidential and other political campaigns; and interviews with presidents Bill Clinton, George W. Bush, and Barack Obama plus countless celebrities. She is a highly sought-after news analyst on CNN and *CBS News*; a commentator for National Public Radio and the *Tom Joyner Morning Show*; and an interviewer for the *New York Times* and the *Washington Post*. She became a columnist at the *Daily Press* (Newport News, VA) to satisfy her urge to be a print journalist.

Such a body of work did not go unnoticed. Columbia University Graduate School of Journalism honored Ciara for her reports on race and ethnicity. She shared that spotlight with CBS's Dan Rather and the producers of *60 Minutes*. *Coastal Virginia Magazine* called her the best

Barbara Ciara interviewing President Barack Obama.

local female TV news anchor in Hampton Roads. In 2008, *Ebony* named her an "*Ebony* Power 150 Organization Leader" for her two-year stint at the helm of the National Association of Black Journalists, the largest minority group of media practitioners in the world. In 2012, she became one of the nation's *HistoryMakers*, a prestigious African American oral and video history project archived at the Library of Congress.

Her broadcast stories earned the Radio and Television News Directors Association's Edward R. Murrow Award, numerous Associated Press and United Press International honors, local awards from the Hampton Roads Black Media Professionals, and Emmy nominations. In 2020, Ciara was inducted in the Virginia Communications Hall of Fame and is most proud of recognition for her stories about people who were voiceless and unseen.

"To be recognized for your work is a wonderful thing. It means people are embracing your work. Giving people a voice through my stories leaves an impact. People need to be reminded that racism is real, but because of privilege, they don't know what it is like to walk in our shoes. The power of the microphone can give people a voice that makes it worth going to work in the morning."

Even though the lifetime of a story is fleeting, Ciara said the most important effect is that it highlights some issue that might "give people an uplift. You have done something to make people feel inspired. They might call to make a donation or help in some way. My job was to tell a story that needs to be told."

Ciara has exceeded that goal, with such projects as "Guilty Until Proven Innocent," a Capitol Regional Emmy Award winner for a series that highlighted how wrongfully imprisoned people felt after they were released. The Emmy-nominated "Letters from the Hood" asked children to write letters to describe life in violent neighborhoods.

Most of all, Ciara said her ambition and her successful career as a nationally known, Emmy Award–winning journalist means never witnessing again the disillusionment in her mother's and family's eyes when she told them she was pregnant at thirteen years old.

"Many of my elders were so disappointed in me. They had such high hopes for me," she said.

"When I compare the consequences of my behavior with their hopes and dreams for me, it was a tough time."

"They told me I was through, my life was over, but I knew it wasn't." Ciara's path to success came after years of missteps—falling, but always picking herself up.

"It was in my mother's DNA. Georgia [Jones] had triple my strength. She should be defined as relentless: fall down, get up, don't whine. She demonstrated through example that failure was not an option."

Ciara admires her mother's determination now, but at 14 she became tired of her mother's authoritative behavior and ran away to New York City with a neighborhood band called Blue Flame to become the next Aretha Franklin, leaving her son, Robbie, behind in Pittsburgh. Although she did not become a singing star, she did not return home with her friends five months later nor did she contact her parents for help.

Fall down, get up, don't whine.

She rented a room at the YWCA, ran out of money, became homeless, slept on the balcony at the Apollo Theater, took makeshift baths at the train station, and got a job at Orange Julius. Terrified at her circumstances, Ciara still knew she was not going back to Pittsburgh.

Instead, she moved to Jersey City, where rent was cheaper and lied about her age (16) to take the Civil Service Examination, which led to a job in a Jersey state welfare office. That job helped her learn clerical skills and obtain her GED. Three years passed as her mother took care of Robbie. Ciara stayed away, only briefly returning to visit before moving to attend the University of Arizona in Tucson.

Ciara said it was her compelling story and the post–civil rights era that opened majority institutions to minorities, which led to her acceptance at the University of Arizona. However, her path toward a career in journalism was made before she left home for New York City when she asked her English teacher why a protest she organized to allow female students to wear pants at Knoxville Junior High School was not

Barbara Ciara with Ed Bradley, the renowned CBS news journalist.

covered by the school paper. The teacher replied, "If you are so smart, why don't you write a story?"

She began writing for the school's newspaper, loved it, and decided to major in journalism at Arizona. However, the local paper in Tucson, which sponsored her scholarship, rejected her stories and job applications because she did not have any experience. She accumulated clips writing for the school paper at Pima Community College, which Ciara also attended because classes there were cheaper, and she could transfer the credits to Arizona.

Although she worked a full-time job as a bank cashier, money was tight, and she could not really count on her working-class parents to send her a lot of money. Ciara said it was the lack of money and her ambition that drove her to leave college in her junior year for the $2.10 full-time job at KZAZ-TV, where she first worked as a part-time production assistant.

Her persistence and pestering of the station's general manager Adelstein, who became her mentor, resulted in progressively better stints as a reporter, assignment editor, producer, noon anchor, and eventually news director (1978). Ciara became the youngest and the first African American woman to hold a management title at a commercial television station in the Southwest.

"I didn't have a college degree, but I wasn't going to let that stop me. Peter Jennings and many others didn't have college degrees. All my training was on the job.

Barbara Ciara proudly holds her 2021 Emmy Award.

"My first on-the-air job was mortifying. It was a nightmare. I had my Angela Davis afro. There was a look of fright on my face. I was robotic. But they were really interested in me, so they gave me a time slot after the late, late movie went off. I did a five-minute update of the news, a rip-and-read of the AP headlines. Goodnight and that was it."

As her career took off, Ciara unsuccessfully tried to move her son, Robbie, to Arizona. Her mother resisted and threatened legal action. She said Jones raised her child not as a grandson, but as if he was her child. Although they eventually agreed to share custody, it was the second time she had a major disagreement with her mother.

In many ways, Ciara's personal life has never met the success of her professional life. Robbie never lived with her on a permanent basis. She is twice divorced.

Fall down, get up, don't whine.

"For every choice you make, there is a consequence. I have learned to make wiser choices. In 1985, I had the perfect man, the perfect house, the perfect cat. By 1992, I still had the cat." The cat comment is consummate Barbara Ciara, whose quick wit and ability to make anyone in her presence laugh help shield her when off-camera.

"I was fully focused on my career," she said of her failed marriages. "Employers weren't interested in my family or personal obligations. Those were hard lessons to learn that a career is not everything.

"I used to have doubts about my life. I was frustrated I couldn't do all the things I wanted to do. But when I consider the sum total of everything I have experienced, at the end of the day, I realize there is more to life than a career. I want to do things to make myself happy.

"My whole life I have taken disadvantages and turned them into advantages. Kids used to tease me because of my high forehead. I began wearing hairstyles that highlighted my forehead. I am flawed like most people, but I have no patience for family or people who whine about their circumstances. There is no value in whining. Make a game plan and move forward."

As she approaches the waning years of her career, Ciara said she will not be sad to leave the spotlight behind. Her work to give voice to her community, to work with those who are less fortunate, will continue. Most important is the monetary and oral legacy she wants to leave her grandchildren and great-grandchildren.

Ciara said they will have funds to go to college, and she wants them to learn from knowing her story—how life threw her curves and she made homeruns.

When the camera lights fade away from Ciara's face for the last time, when her last signature sign off "Thanks for the company" is aired, Ciara knows her late mother is pleased by the life she made for herself.

She refused to stay down and never whined.

Cathy M. Jackson, Ph.D., is an associate professor of journalism at Norfolk State University who previously worked for daily newspapers in Michigan and Florida. She lives in Norfolk, Virginia.

Chapter 11

Sandra C. Dillard

Bright Lights, Big Cities Fuel Passion for Journalism—From the Classroom to World Stages, Creativity Played a Leading Role

By Michelle Fitzhugh-Craig

As Sandra Dillard gathered with the other forty-three journalists at the Sheraton Park Hotel, on December 12, 1975, in Washington, D.C., she knew she was witnessing something special. The group had convened to discuss forming a national organization whose purpose would be to provide quality programming and services for all Black journalists working in newsrooms throughout the country.

"We needed an advocacy group; we needed a group for people like me. I was sitting out in Denver by myself," Dillard remembered. She was divorced at the time with a 12-year-old son and had a lot on the line.

"I'm risking my job, but I really think this is important, so I'm just going to go ahead and risk it," she told herself.

Since that day, Dillard has proudly served as one of the founding members of the National Association of Black Journalists. The group, which currently boasts around 4,000 members, has diligently worked for diversity and inclusion of Black media professionals and to increase the number of minorities in newsrooms across the country.

"I'm so proud and impressed about what the group has grown to be," Dillard said.

But the reality was that racism—and sometimes in Dillard's case, sexism—was a problem that she dealt with often long before she even entered a newsroom.

Dillard's early years were spent in San Francisco and then Sacramento. She was always interested in journalism, even though her mother and grandmother were both educators. At age 9, she was writing short stories about the local Camp Fire Girls troop for her neighborhood paper.

Shortly after her early writing experience, Dillard moved with her family to Denver in 1950, where she has lived ever since. One of her favorite memories includes being the first and only Black person ever to represent Colorado/Wyoming in the Scripps National Spelling Bee at age 13 in 1951. Sponsored by the local newspaper, she was sent to Washington, D.C., with a chaperone. This experience proved to be more profound than she could ever imagine. First, many strings had to be pulled so that she could stay in the famous Willard Hotel with the other contestants. Finally, she was given a room with no windows and was the only contestant with no roommate.

In the nation's capital, she and another contestant decided to take advantage of the free movie passes given to the students. Dropped off by their chaperones, Dillard was denied entrance because she was Black (the other student was white); the two had to walk back to their hotel in the dark and without supervision. She said as her time there continued, the constant "photo ops" with senators and other VIPs stirred something deep inside.

Coverage of her spelling bee experience did not include her treatment, but instead focused on light-hearted features about her discovering the number of steps at the Washington Monument. She made it to the final rounds but did not win.

"This is what I want to write about," Dillard said. "I wanted to tell them [people] about what happened to me at the hotel and [at the movies]. That's when I started suspecting there weren't enough real stories about us . . . about Black people."

Dillard continued to see and experience racism and unfair treatment in her life. While writing for her high school paper, she lost the editor's position to a white boy. Still, she persevered and earned an academic full ride to the University of Denver where she continued to feed her passion for writing by working on the newspaper and yearbook staffs. She graduated in 1959 with a degree in elementary education and a minor in journalism and started teaching at age 21. Dillard decided to study education instead of journalism, which she minored in, because choices then were limited for most Black women with college degrees, who mostly became librarians, teachers, or social workers. And as much as she enjoyed journalism, Dillard did not think she could make a living doing it.

After graduating, Dillard starting teaching at age 21, instructing second and third graders at Denver's Ebert Elementary School. The following year she married and moved to Washington, D.C., and taught at Powell Elementary School. Returning to Denver a few years later, she taught third grade at the mostly white Newlon Elementary School. When the school year ended, in 1968—two months after the assassination of the Rev. Dr. Martin Luther King, Jr.—she headed to the University of

California at Santa Barbara to participate in The Summer Institute in Black Repertory Theatre. The fellowship program, sponsored by the U.S. Office of Education, Arts and Humanities Institute, selected 41 Black teachers and college students who were interested in teaching theater and performing arts that focused on Black issues. The goal was to tighten the cultural lag among Blacks in drama at a time when traditional barriers were being lowered. During the summer institute, participants performed plays and musicals, including *A Land Beyond the River*, playwright Loften Mitchell's drama based on Joseph DeLaine's historic South Carolina court case, which became one of the five court cases to end segregation in public schools. Dillard recalled that August Wilson, who won Pulitzer Prizes for two of his works, *Fences* and *The Piano Lesson*, was a playwright-in-residence during the program. The work of the institute's staff and students is captured in the book, *The Black Teacher and the Dramatic Arts: A Dialogue, Bibliography, and Anthology*. And while she may not have known it then, the theater workshop proved pivotal in Dillard's later career as a newspaper theater critic.

When the institute ended, Dillard returned to Denver and taught another year of elementary school before transferring to Manual High to teach English and drama. She was inspired to get her master's degree in theater, and went back to the University of California at Santa Barbara a year later. While there, she became founding editor of a newspaper, *Black Vibrations*, for Black students.

In 1972, shortly before completing her master's, Dillard heard about the Summer Program for Minority Journalists at Columbia University. She applied and one of its instructors was Robert C. Maynard, who later established the Maynard Institute for Journalism Education. She said Maynard was hesitant to select her as a fellow because she already "had a career as a teacher.

Dillard stood her ground. "Yes, I was a teacher, but it was not the career I wanted," she explained. "I was a good teacher, but I didn't want to be a teacher."

She became one of 12 out of 500 applicants selected for the program. Participants were guaranteed a reporting job at a newspaper after completing the program. The *Denver Post*, her hometown newspaper, agreed that Dillard could participate in the program under its auspices. She described Maynard, who died in August 1993, as "a masterful teacher and fascinating storyteller."

When the summer program ended, Dillard became a full-time reporter for the *Denver Post*, Colorado's largest newspaper, and the first Black woman to work at a daily newspaper in Colorado. The newspaper had a strong reputation, having won its first of several Pulitzer Prizes eight years before Dillard began working there in September 1972. The University of Denver's student newspaper ran a front-page photo of its successful alumna.

Dillard was finally doing what she had started as a child. She covered several different beats at the *Denver Post*—including fashion, suburban government, education, Denver City Hall, political races, feature stories and politics; with the latter, she covered Congress from the paper's Washington, D.C., bureau in 1979. Her favorite beat was being the night reporter—that was until she was able to fulfill her not-so-guilty pleasure for the theater.

After 18 years at the paper, she became the *Denver Post*'s theater critic. Dillard spent the next eleven years covering local, national and international theater and producing her Sunday column until she took an early retirement in 2001. Awards and honors include her selection as a Eugene O'Neill critic fellow, a prestigious program at Yale University, in 1990. She was the first Black selected for the program that provided intensive critical writing training. During the fellowship, participants saw plays and worked with playwrights. "That added to my confidence and further honed my skills," she recalled.

During her years as a theater critic, Dillard was an emcee in the late 1990s for the Unique Lives and Experiences at the Buell Theater which included honorees Maya Angelou, Shirley McLaine and Julie Andrews.

She also spoke at several theater conferences throughout the country and has been quoted on the covers of several theater books.

Her honors and awards include a Denver Newspaper Guild Award for Excellence in Journalism for Commentary; Alliance for Colorado Theater Service to the Profession,1994; Colorado Association of Black Journalists Lifetime Achievement, 1997; and Team Pulitzer in 1999 for the Columbine High School shootings.

Despite Dillard's success, racism and sexism were issues she often encountered. Early in her newspaper days, the secretary of her managing editor asked whether she could put Dillard's picture on top of a nude body photo because, "Every time you come down here, he always makes a comment about your build," the secretary said. Dillard was shocked at the comment, even more so because it came from a woman. She did not run into a lot of these situations and not knowing newsroom politics, was unsure of how to handle the sexist request. So she simply told the woman, "No."

Another incident involved not being allowed to include a photo of a Black man who had been whipped, which seemed sensible to run with her review of a play about the Omaha, Nebraska race riot of 1919. The riot occurred after Black workers were hired to replace striking white workers at an Omaha meatpacking plant.

There also were occasional sources who refused to talk with her because of her race.

"Well, if you want this story in the paper you have to talk to me," Dillard told one convention chairwoman. Another incident occurred when she was assigned to a woman whose grandmother made her enter the home, located in Denver's country club district, through the back door.

One of the most impactful and blatant incidents of racism she experienced occurred when she was covering a workshop for the city's newest graduating police cadets. She overheard one of the rookies say, "The first thing I'm going to do is kill Lauren Watson"—referring to the Black Panthers' Denver chapter president—and Dillard's brother.

Truth Tellers: *The Power and Presence of Black Women Journalists Since 1960*

"They wouldn't let me run it," she said. "They told me to 'just write about facts' from the meeting."

Dillard wrote the facts and more, including reports on poor conditions at Denver's East Side Health Center, racial inequality in Denver Public Schools, and the Black woman's take on the Women's Liberation Movement. "I got all the space I needed for the comments and photos of about a dozen well-known women from Denver's Black community," she said in a 2009 National Association of Black Journalists Founders Task Force Report.

Dillard's role as a founding member of NABJ kept her active in the Colorado Association of Black Journalists, including a stint as the chapter's president. She also taught for two summers at the Institute for Journalism Education at the University of California at Berkeley, which she said in an NABJ Founders Task Force article "is now renamed The Maynard Institute." Her advice to aspiring journalists in that same publication is simple:

"Ask for what you want but you have to be prepared," she said, noting how she would volunteer for election night coverage, which ultimately led to work in the newspaper's Washington bureau and occasionally covering the White House.

She also advises young journalists to "pick your battles—you don't want to be known as a difficult person"—and to position themselves. Her selection as the *Post*'s theater critic came after writing as a backup critic for two years. When the critic decided to attend law school, she was the natural choice with "not only my M.A. in theater but a substantial collection of theater clips." As a result, she was the American Theater Critics Association's first Black member, led a National Theater Critics conference in Denver, and helped secure the 1998 Regional Tony Award for the Denver Center Theatre Company.

In her farewell column, Dillard wrote:

It's been a wonderful journey. What other career lets you experience parties at the White House and the inside of the Colorado State Penitentiary? I had the chance to talk to people as varied as presidents, advice columnists, actors, actresses, coroners, designers, convicts, movie stars, athletes, fashion designers, theater directors and opera singers. The job also gave me the chance to travel to New York, twice yearly to see major Broadway shows and interview the stars of shows coming to Denver. I also attended shows in London and Montreal, and several of the 50 states. Where else but in journalism could you observe surgeries and autopsies; or cover fires, murders and events from a state funeral to the 1979 signing of the Camp David peace accord in the White House Rose Garden?

"Also keep learning," she said, adding that she often gave up vacation time to take writing and editing courses.

Before COVID-19, Dillard spent her days traveling, shopping, dining with friends, and spending time with her third husband, Warren Scott. Her son, Alton, lives nearby and works as communications manager for Denver's Office of the Clerk and Recorder. She also has spent time during her retirement volunteering as a reading teacher at her alma mater, Manual High School in Denver, and worked as a clerk for the Colorado senate.

Although people often suggest that Dillard write a book about her life as a journalist, she has no interest in doing so. But she admits that she is still hopeful for inclusive newsrooms everywhere and more important, the continuation of the hard copy daily newspaper, along with NABJ's continuing commitment to Black journalists.

"I hope NABJ continues to grow in its influence," Dillard said. "My concern of course, is I take the paper every day . . . and I keep waiting for the day it doesn't come anymore. I really, really believe people don't realize how important it is."

Michelle Fitzhugh-Craig is president of Exceptional Women in Publishing. Her publication credits include Living in the Moment: A Guide to Living a Full and Spiritual Life *and* Chicken Soup for the African American Woman's Soul. *She lives in Oakland, California.*

PART 3

Changing How Communities Are Covered

Chapter 12

Cassandra Spratling

Chronicling the Events and Sacrifices of Everyday People—
Detroit Is Center Stage for Covering the Extraordinary and
Ordinary for Forty Years

By Cathy Gant Hill

To celebrate the fortieth anniversary of the Montgomery Bus Boycott in 1995, *Detroit Free Press* journalist Cassandra Spratling interviewed domestic workers who walked to their jobs during the 381-day boycott rather than ride the segregated buses of Montgomery. In a rare moment, the writer cried as one woman explained her nightly ritual for more than a year: Epsom-salt footbaths to ease her pain.

Spratling's decision to write about the not-so-famous protesters instead of the iconic Rosa Parks who, in the years following her historic

1955 bus boycott for civil rights, moved from Alabama to Detroit, was intentional. As much as she adored Parks, she knew that the courage and strength displayed by hundreds of others seeking change was equally important.

"I will never forget being in that woman's living room," Spratling said. "She still had the basin where she would soak her feet. I said, 'How did you do that'? I felt like I wanted to *kiss* her feet. She did this for me. I wouldn't have been there interviewing her had she not done that."

As with many journalists, particularly African American journalists of the post–civil rights era, Spratling, who retired from the *Detroit Free Press* in 2015 is rankled mightily by injustice. While reading Malcolm X's autobiography in high school, she was outraged by a white teacher dismissing Malcolm Little's ambition to become a lawyer because he was "Negro."

"He was smart, a leader," Spratling said of the young Malcolm. "He had all the attributes that would have made him an outstanding lawyer. I remember being so upset. Malcolm inspired me.

"I said, 'I'm going to be what I want to be. For my mother and father.'"

Spratling's determination to report and write stories that revealed the injustice often shouldered by poor, working-class or everyday people who happened to be Black possibly was sparked the day she was born. She points out that her birth date, December 1, 1955, is the same day that Rosa Parks ignited the Montgomery Bus Boycott by refusing to give up her seat to make room for white passengers.

"It has stayed with me pretty much all of my life," said Spratling, who learned of the connection as a child. "In no way would I ever compare what I've done to Rosa Parks's legacy, but knowing that I was born on that day has always said to me that I needed to do something of service that lifts her struggle. And not just her struggle, but our struggle. I've been grateful as a journalist that I've been able to do that."

So immense is Spratling's gratitude that she celebrated her 60th birthday by writing "Countdown to 60," a series of stories that included her bicycle ride from Selma to Montgomery to mark the 50th anniversary of the Voting Rights March in 2015. The series resulted in a 2016 Salute to Excellence Award from the National Association of Black Journalists.

Yet, Spratling remains proudest of those stories about ordinary people—like her parents doing extraordinary things or participating in extraordinary events. Her now-deceased parents, Annie Lou and Fletcher Spratling, migrated North from Alabama for better opportunities than were available in the Jim Crow South. Her father barely made it to middle school, stopping at seventh grade to help his sharecropping family. Her mother worked cleaning other people's homes for part of her life. They emphasized education for their children.

"Knowing where they came from, I always felt a responsibility and a real determination to do better," said Spratling, the only daughter of five children. "It was my gift to do for them what they could not do."

Full of questions and dreams, Spratling's imagination about people's lives sprouted early. She grew up hearing and reading civil rights history that included the remarkable achievements of African Americans, both famous and lesser known. The list of subjects she has interviewed or covered reads like a twentieth- and twenty-first-century roll call of famous Black people, many of them identifiable by only one name: Rosa, Mandela, Angelou, Aretha, Oprah.

Ultimately, Spratling, the self-described "Black girl from the Jeffries Projects," proved time and again that her greatest stories for the *Detroit Free Press* were gleaned from the events and sacrifices of hardworking people like the ones she studied as a child.

In the beginning, though, Spratling thought that journalism described creative writing. Spratling was introduced to journalism at Detroit's Mackenzie High School. A standout English student, Spratling's lower-grade teachers encouraged her to take journalism classes in the upper grades.

She almost dropped the class because of her misconceptions about journalism. Maxine Perry, the journalism teacher, assured Spratling that not only would she be writing nonfiction, but that she could learn to do it with as much flair and style as the young Spratling saw in this confident, nattily dressed educator.

"It was at the end of that class that I knew that I wanted to be a journalist," Spratling said. "It gave me a license to talk to people and to ask questions and to write."

She became editor of the high school paper, the *Mackenzie Dial*. She liked the title, along with what it entailed. "I always enjoyed the editing and writing. Never good at layout and design. I knew I wanted to go to Michigan State because it had a Black newspaper at the time, the *Grapevine Journal*. I knew the editor and I knew I could work on that paper. At Michigan State, I ended up working on the *Grapevine* and helped start another Black paper, the *People's Choice*, which covered issues such as college life and events directly relevant to Black students. I'm guessing it was my third year. I just felt like I was doing what I wanted to do . . . write and edit stories relevant to African American community."

While at Michigan State, Spratling accepted an internship at *Better Homes and Garden* magazine in Des Moines, Iowa. It was very eye-opening in a lot of ways.

"It was interesting to see how a magazine works. We'd have photo shoots at amazing houses. Up until then I'd never seen houses like that. I didn't know people lived like that. Kitchens that looked like that could have been in somebody's restaurant. Also, what stood out was how segregated communities were. In Des Moines, there was 'the block' an area where Black people lived. To see Black people—there were two other Black interns at the magazine—but to see other Black people, I'd have to go to 'the block.'"

After graduating from Michigan State in 1977, Spratling's first full-time job was covering the night police beat for the *South Bend Tribune* in Indiana. About 220 miles west of Detroit and with a roughly 25 percent African American population, South Bend was not exactly a world away from the Motor City, but it was different enough that Spratling stood out, especially at work.

"I was the only African American woman there," Spratling recalled. "There was only one Black man there. I did feel isolated sometimes, but I made it less so by becoming actively involved in the Black community of South Bend."

She worked for the South Bend paper until entering the graduate journalism program at the University of Michigan in 1979, and she interned at the *Detroit Free Press* during the summer of 1980. The internship enabled her to get closer to her long-term goal of working for her hometown paper full time.

When she was hired by the *Free Press* in 1981, Spratling realized she was back at her proving ground, basking in the hometown newsprint and ink, and soaking up wisdom from role models and mentors, which included two legendary African American women journalists: the late Susan Watson, the first columnist and the first woman editor at the *Free Press*; and Betty DeRamus, author, retired reporter and columnist, who worked for the *Free Press* and the *Detroit News*.

"Their writing was just so powerful and on point," Spratling said. "They really inspired me, to see them, to know them, to see what was possible." They never responded to the old tropes often posed to people of color, *Are you Black first or a journalist first?* Spratling's role models proved that they were both: using the power of their words to advocate for African American causes and conditions but also taking power to task, among white and African American leadership.

"I will forever be grateful for the example that they set in the newsroom," Spratling said of DeRamus and Watson. "They weren't grinning and hiding. They were being who they were." They were Black and proud. They weren't trying to assimilate. They were writers who reflected the community from which they came and that they cared about."

Spratling, whose positions included assistant entertainment editor and assistant city editor, is also known for authenticity. Her attention to detail brings her stories off pages and into people's psyches. In addition to the NABJ Salute to Excellence Award, Spratling has won awards for writing and reporting, including the School Bell Award from the Michigan Press Association and the Spirit of Diversity Award from the Wayne State University Journalism Institute for Media Diversity.

Communion with other journalists, particularly through the National Association of Black Journalists (NABJ), also helped propel Spratling's career. She recalls NABJ's founding member, the late Vernon Jarrett, telling an audience at Michigan State about the group's humble start in 1975.

"He said when they first organized that they could have met in a telephone booth, their numbers were so small," Spratling said, laughing at the memory. "He was a giant in journalism." Jarrett himself had a long career at the *Chicago Sun Times* and formed the NAACP's Act-So program.

If meeting Jarrett was inspiring, interacting with NABJ progeny at her first convention in 1982 in Detroit set her aflame.

"I was feeling such pride and excitement that there were all these Black journalists like me who were doing what they do," Spratling said.

Spratling retired from the *Free Press* in 2015, but she hasn't stopped writing. Still equipped with a license to probe, she is a freelance writer who enjoys detailing others' experiences. Indeed, her own experiences have intersected with history and the ancestors in a way that makes readers laugh, cry and revel in the words she writes for the *Detroit Free Press*, *National Geographic*, and *Visit Detroit*.

She advises young people entering journalism to "read great writers, both fiction and nonfiction, but especially nonfiction. Write stories that matter to you and your community. Don't limit yourself. Seek opportunities that challenge and stretch you and always know that you are worthy and capable of great work. Surround yourself, both personally and professionally, with people who will encourage and support you."

Cathy Gant Hill is a freelance editor, writer, and educator who worked fourteen years as a reporter covering arts, county government, and consumer affairs for the Greensboro (NC) News & Record. She lives in Greensboro, North Carolina.

Chapter 13

Mae Israel

Speaking, with Authority and Passion, for Black Lives—
Overcoming Speech Impediment, Racism, and Sexism to
Find Career Success

Mae Israel's pilgrimage to the *Washington Post* in 1989 began in seventh grade at Lincoln Junior High School in Greensboro, North Carolina. An attentive student, Israel devoured works by James Baldwin and other Black writers, thanks to an uncle who gave her books as Christmas gifts.

Her English teacher, the adviser to the school's newspaper, noticed that Israel also enjoyed writing and suggested that she join the *Lincoln Echo*, the school newspaper.

Once she began writing for her school newspaper, she latched onto the idea of becoming a journalist, an unexpected career choice for someone who speaks with a stutter.

Truth Tellers: *The Power and Presence of Black Women Journalists Since 1960*

"I fell in love with language, and I knew then that I would become a journalist," she said. "In high school, I really began to understand the power of the written word. I wanted to work as a newspaper reporter because I thought there were stories that needed to be written."

Israel wanted to write stories about the need for social change and life in the Black community. Although she was too young to write about the push for equality surrounding her during the late 1950s and early1960s, she was aware of the impact of those stories unfolding in Greensboro, a midsize Southern city shaped by textile mills and cigarette manufacturing.

Nonviolent sits-ins at Woolworth's department store lunch counter thrust the region into the national spotlight on February 1, 1960. Black students at North Carolina A&T State University led the protests with demands to be served food in the same place they spent money for school and personal items. Joining these students were women from the Black, all female Bennett College in Greensboro, along with students from the white University of North Carolina at Greensboro.

Widespread busing and public school desegregation followed the students' success in integrating lunch counters, although such steps came nearly a decade after the U.S. Supreme Court ruled in *Brown v. Board of Education of Topeka* that state laws establishing racial segregation in public schools were unconstitutional.

After moving his family from rural Robeson County to Greensboro in the mid-1950s, Israel's father, Samuel, worked odd jobs until he was hired at Lorillard Tobacco Company, a prominent cigarette manufacturing company in the city's East End. His wife, Mae, was a domestic worker until securing work in one of the blue-collar factories. In 1957, Samuel and Mae purchased a house on East Florida Street, one of the few segregated areas where Blacks were allowed to purchase homes. The modest, brick houses were built next to the city's sewage treatment plant.

"In the summer that smell was horrible," she said.

Still, buying a home spelled progress—albeit slow progress.

"In the 1950s and 1960s, if you were able to buy a house you were happy to do so," Israel. "Once Black people got into leadership

Mae Israel

positions, the city began to build parks and community centers" in Black neighborhoods.

As a member of the NAACP, Samuel Israel often talked about the civil rights movement and other challenges facing Black people. As she grew older, Mae Israel, the oldest of her parents' four daughters, began to grasp the significance of their discussions and the adverse impact of living in a segregated society.

"I saw what was happening on television. When Woolworth's happened, I was so young, and I don't remember hearing much about them [protesters] at that age. But in junior high and high school, I learned about it."

A major lesson Israel witnessed was student protests at Greensboro's predominantly Black Dudley High School on May 21, 1969.

Israel, a tenth grader at Dudley saw hundreds of students walk out of their classrooms to protest school officials' failure to acknowledge Claude Barnes as student body president after Barnes won the seat by a write-in vote. No reason was given for the decision, according to published reports, but Dudley's students believed that Barnes's reputation as a student activist and member of GAPP (Greensboro Association of Poor People) directed the officials' actions. The protests spread to A&T's campus and National Guardsmen soon joined the fray. Amid the chaos, tragedy struck.

"It was horrible," Israel said. "Student protesters were tear-gassed, white authorities from downtown took over the authority of Dudley. They shut down Dudley and A&T. In the midst of it, an A&T student was killed."

Israel left school during the protests and did not participate in the struggles. She attended Dudley for one year before transferring to the predominantly white Page High School, where she felt the available academic resources could strengthen her plans to attend college.

"I had gone to mostly segregated schools and had a lot of excellent teachers," said Israel. "I heard from them over and over, 'Strive to do your best. Study hard. Work hard. Learn how to deal with a white society that doesn't want to deal with you. Aim to do your best.' I heard that over and over."

Israel thrived at Page, where she worked on the newspaper staff and became one of the paper's editors during her senior year. Her goal of attending college was met in 1971 when she was accepted at several colleges but chose the University of North Carolina at Chapel Hill because of its highly regarded journalism school. She wrote for the *Black Ink*, a newsletter that became a monthly newspaper and was taken seriously by the school's administration.

"You had African American students at a majority university, and we wanted to make sure that we received a fair shake," explained Israel. "Back then it was a very strong newspaper, and we helped to make it relevant by dealing with diversity and issues that we felt weren't being dealt with in the *Daily Tar Heel*," the school's student-run newspaper.

Israel never worked for the *Daily Tar Heel* but her work as an editor for *Black Ink* and a work-study position as a reporter for UNC's news bureau enabled her to write about visiting luminaries, such as poet Nikki Giovanni and activist Jamil Abdullah Al-Amin, formerly known as H. Rap Brown. News clips about the speakers and other university activities subsequently helped Israel land an internship at the *Greensboro Daily News*, where she worked for two summers.

Israel paused when asked about her overall experience at Chapel Hill. "We learned what we were made of because it wasn't easy. When we walked into UNC in 1971, we were the largest group of African American freshmen ever. UNC is now more diverse. But we had to deal with professors who thought we should not be there.

"We were dealing with social issues of being young, African American students at the dawn of affirmative action. It was a time when we were all trying to figure out how we would fit."

In 1973, Israel broke ground as one of five charter members of the first Black sorority on campus, a chapter of Delta Sigma Theta Sorority, Inc., which was founded in 1913 at Howard University and began expanding to predominantly white universities in the 1970s as Black student enrollment increased. She also was involved in the Black Student Movement, which pushed for equitable treatment of Black students and for the university to allocate student funds to support its activities as it did other campus organizations.

Israel graduated from college in 1975 and began working as a reporter at the *Greensboro Daily News*. There, her reporting experiences ranged from covering festivals to city government, neighborhood protests to school board meetings. But what perhaps was one of the most pivotal stories of her young career occurred on November 3, 1979. During a Communist Workers Party parade in support of a union for mostly Black textile mill workers, violence erupted when Ku Klux Klansmen and American Nazi Party members showed up with guns. By the time the bloody shootout in the city's Morningside Homes public housing community ended, five Communist Workers Party members—four men and one woman—were dead. The shooting had echoes of the Dudley High School protests that ended with the shooting death of an A&T student a decade earlier. This time Israel did not walk away from the chaos: she covered it.

"It was scary," Israel recalls of the shooting that many of Greensboro's Black residents still consider as a not-too-subtle tactic to keep them in their place. "My understanding is that Greensboro police knew something would happen but did nothing to prevent it. That was one of the biggest stories to hit Greensboro. I just remember really wanting to make sure the story was being told right . . . how people were reacting, community sentiment, and the impact. I wanted to be sure that it was told honestly."

(In subsequent state criminal and federal civil rights court trials, the KKK and Nazis were acquitted by all-white juries for their roles in the massacre. In a 1985 civil trial, a North Carolina jury found two Greensboro police officers, six Klansmen and Nazis liable for the "wrongful death" of one of the CWP demonstrators who was killed and ordered the city of Greensboro to pay nearly $400,000 in damages.)

"I just remember that after that, particularly because of the reaction of the Greensboro police, there was a lot of animosity in the community."

Greensboro's city council was in denial about the massacre and failed to formally apologize for its role until four decades later on August 15, 2017, and October 6, 2020.

Israel was long gone by the time a Greensboro Truth and Reconciliation Commission issued a 2006 report on the massacre and city council's apologies. After being contacted by a newspaper editor in Charlotte, she left Greensboro in 1980 for the *Charlotte Observer*, a highly respected newspaper about eighty miles from Greensboro. Before leaving Greensboro, she spoke with one of *Daily News*'s editors about the Charlotte job offer.

"I remember when I went in and told him the *Charlotte Observer* had offered me a job as a reporter, he told me I would not succeed [at a larger newspaper] because of my stutter. And I said to myself, 'You do not know me.' I always knew if I worked hard I could do it. But here is this white man who thinks he is going to dictate my life. He probably thought, 'She works for us and does a good job for us.' But the idea that I would go to work for the [larger] Charlotte paper? I think he had put me in a box. I said to him, 'I can do this job.'"

Israel has spoken with a stutter since she was a child and over the years learned to manage it through speech therapy.

"No one knows why people stutter," she said. "But in my experience as a person who has always stuttered, there are times when it's more obvious. But it was an issue that people knew about.

Israel's self-confidence was a crucial ally beyond newsrooms; she relied on it in encounters with people in power, communities she covered and when facing everyday adversaries.

Even in Charlotte, where she considered her new colleagues to be "a decent group of folks," Israel was ever mindful that "whenever she walked in the door you have to prove yourself every day, especially for a young woman."

Newsrooms are notorious for larger-than-life personalities and huge egos. At times, working for any news organization can be akin to hazing, particularly if certain people believed you shouldn't be there. Israel encountered such behavior more than once.

"People would say [negative] things [to you], and you always felt like you had to fight, fight, fight," she said. "When big stories were being discussed, I noticed that my name wasn't on the list, and I'd have to go in and ask why. I was always having to speak up. You were always in a situation where if you didn't speak up you were just left out."

Even involvement with the National Association of Black Journalists drew fire, which was started in the mid-1970s to advocate for and offer educational opportunities to Black journalists. During its early years, newsroom editors "wanted to know why we needed a group like this." For Israel and countless other Black journalists, NABJ has been vital in their career growth and development. "I remember [a time] when we went to NABJ [conventions], we seriously went to workshops that were useful and helpful. It was very much an anchor as we were finding our way around and learning to navigate the newsroom; NABJ was there as a sort of silent partner. It was an advocate. I think that most of us who started out in the 1970s were in NABJ."

After nearly a decade in Charlotte where she covered the area's growth, development and transportation beats, along with a stint as assistant government editor, Israel wanted to grow professionally and have more of an impact in journalism. She left the *Observer* in 1989 for the *Washington Post* where she was hired as an assistant metro editor to focus on coverage in suburban Virginia, and later moved to editing coverage in adjacent Maryland. She quickly learned that the *Washington Post* was a more intense and competitive environment. Yet, she gained a deep sense of satisfaction from her work and credits the job for helping her develop strong negotiation skills. "As an editor, I was able to get some stories done that made a difference. I was getting feedback from the community."

When Israel arrived at the *Post*, the newspaper was "rebounding" after several Black men and women reporters in 1972 protested the newspaper's discriminatory practices involving assignments, salaries, and promotions. The employees, known as the Metro Seven, filed a landmark Equal Employment Opportunity Commission complaint against the newspaper. Although the case was not pursued in federal court, it was followed by a similar complaint by women. That case was settled in 1980.

"When I was struggling in Greensboro, others [Black journalists at other newspapers] were struggling, too," said Israel, in reference to discriminatory practices encountered by Black reporters in newsrooms throughout the country. "As a result of the lawsuit, the *Post* had started to try to make the staff more diverse."

Israel encourages young people who are interested in journalism to heed the advice of the teachers and role models who helped guide her while growing up: Strive to do your best. Study hard. Work hard.

"For young people interested in this field, this is an industry in desperate need of people who want to ensure that our society still gets a diverse message," she said. "I think it's still an industry where we need young Black women who really want to speak out for a range of thoughts and ideas. It is not an industry for the faint of heart. It's an industry where you have to reach deep within yourself, where you have to have an essential belief in yourself to make a contribution, and where you have to fight to be willing to do that. If you can walk out of a newsroom standing, you can deal with anything."

Now retired but working part-time as an independent journalist in the Charlotte area, Israel declared she has no regrets.

"Would I have done it all over, would I do it over? Yes. Because there is no way to describe what it has meant to be a part of peoples' lives—to get them to talk, to be able to be a part of sharing so many different sorts of stories. There's no better way. I can't think of anything more interesting. No day is ever the same. Having the opportunity to have first access to the news is huge."

Chapter 14

Felecia Henderson

A Voice for the Community—A Defining Moment
Inspires Renewed Purpose

By Sadeqa Johnson

A turning point, one that shaped her future, occurred a few months into Felecia Henderson's job at the *Louisville Courier-Journal*. *Charlie & Co.* was a new sitcom that aired on CBS in the fall of 1985. The TV critic for the newspaper wrote in his review that *Charlie & Co.* was so patterned after *The Cosby Show* that even the stars, Gladys Knight and Phylicia Rashad, looked alike. Henderson was floored, knowing that the stars did not favor. She went to the managing editor and told him the remark was offensive and that it implied that all Black people look alike. The editor was embarrassed and thanked her for pointing it out.

"That was a defining moment for me. I knew right then and there that I wanted to be a copy editor," Henderson recalled. "A voice for her community, the person who made sure that the information that went out into the world was accurate."

Henderson's willingness to speak up had been drilled into her as a child. In addition to growing up in a "happy and loving childhood environment," her parents poured into their only child a strong sense of self. She was encouraged to explore all of her interests. She was the first Black cheerleader at Louisville's Iroquois High School, ran track, and was a member of the band, playing both flute and saxophone. When she was in ninth grade, Kentucky's Jefferson County Public Schools district underwent court-ordered busing. As a result, she was among hundreds of students appointed as peer group counselors to help students transition to new schools, mediate conflict, and promote the understanding of differences among all students. "Interestingly, I've realized that work inspired me to continue in that vein professionally."

Despite her many achievements before graduating high school, Henderson was unsure about what she wanted to be when she grew up; she just knew she did not want to follow the women in her family and become a teacher. Teaching and nursing were traditional careers for women at that time, and all the women in her family had earned master's degrees in education. She had three great-aunts who were high school teachers, and her mother and her mother's sister taught high school business education—at Henderson's high school. Surrounded by educators made her crave something different and gave her the passion to embark on a career that would ultimately break the family mold.

At age 12, she got a glimpse of what her future could be like through her older cousin, DeVeen Perry, who was home from Murray State University on spring break. Perry colored Henderson's imagination with details about pledging Delta Sigma Theta sorority and studying to be a radio announcer or TV anchor. Prior to that visit, Henderson had no idea of her area of interest, but her cousin painted a picture so glamorous that she decided to follow in Perry's footsteps.

Felecia Henderson

She had always watched local TV news, but once she decided to pursue the career professionally, she began intentionally watching women at the anchor desk, especially those who looked like her. Monica Kaufman was an anchor on WHAS-TV in Louisville, her hometown, and Henderson watched her religiously every weekend. By the time she reached high school, Pam Moore was the Black female anchor at WHAS-TV and she became her role model, so much so that Henderson's mother, who sponsored the Future Business Leaders of America chapter at her school, invited Pam Moore to speak at the high school's banquet. This landed Henderson a seat right next to her idol where she picked her brain on a career in TV.

When it was time for her to apply for college, Henderson's mind was set on majoring in radio, TV, and journalism, but her practical mother encouraged her to major in music so that she would have a teacher's certificate to fall back on. To satisfy her burning desires and her mother's wishes, Henderson went off to Murray State University, in Murray, Kentucky, as a double major in broadcast journalism and music.

As a sophomore, she took her first copyediting class and fell in love with writing headlines, which summarized a story in five words or less. By her junior year, she was the production chief of the *Murray State News*, the university newspaper. A few of her broadcast professors cautioned that her raspy voice would keep her off the air, but that did not discourage Henderson at all. She had her heart set on running the show. When graduation rolled around, she knew that she wanted a job in copyediting. She just did not know how she was going to get her foot in the door.

After earning her degree, she returned home to Louisville, Kentucky, and applied to every single job posting at the *Courier-Journal*, the city's daily morning newspaper, leaving no stone unturned. Her tenacity impressed the human resources director who sat down with Henderson for over an hour to help pinpoint her interest. Within a month, she was offered a job as a clerk editor, an entry-level position for young journalists, in the Neighborhood section. She held the position from 1984 to 1987. On the weekends, she moonlighted as a weekend radio announcer at

WLOU-AM. Ultimately, she knew print journalism was the more stable of the two and a pivotal moment at the *Courier-Journal* clinched her commitment to her field.

In 1987, Henderson was ready to take her career to the next level and applied for the Minority Editing Program at the University of Arizona, sponsored by the Maynard Institute for Journalism Education, the nation's oldest nonprofit dedicated to training and diversifying America's newsrooms. Even though the *Courier-Journal* would not sponsor her, nor hold her job for her, Henderson knew that she had to leave.

After the Maynard program, she landed at the *Cincinnati Post* for two years. Because her fiancé, Angelo B. Henderson, was still in Louisville, they decided to look for a newspaper without a nepotism policy where they could both work as journalists. He found his dream job in Detroit, and when he told her she said, "Detroit, I don't want to go to Detroit, for real?" She later admitted, "It's one of those places that grows on you, and thirty years later I'm still there."

Henderson moved on to the *Detroit News* where she spent ten years as a copy editor and page designer. At the time, she thought her career was going to be in design. Her first editor at the *Cincinnati Post* exposed her to design, which does not require an art or photography background. To be a designer, you need to be able to effectively blend typography, photography, and graphics to tell a story. Page design gave her the ability to be involved in images selected to accompany new stories to ensure diversity as well as fair and accurate representation in the newspaper. She was among a handful of Black female design editors in the country, but in 1993, she was tapped to lead a new section of the paper called *On Detroit*. With this position, her reach expanded. She had a staff of four reporters, and *On Detroit* became the feel-good section of the paper, highlighting good things that happened in Detroit that never received the spotlight. "At the time, Detroit was just coming off of a *Primetime Live* special that portrayed Detroit in a negative light. The city still had one of the highest

Felecia Henderson

Felecia Henderson at the Detroit News copy desk in 1991.

crime rates in the country, and random fires occurring a few days before Halloween worsened the city's image. So, this section showed the other side of Detroit." Henderson worked on the section for six years.

During the course of her very busy career, she was married for twenty-four years to Angelo Henderson, who won a Pulitzer Prize in 1999 while working at the *Wall Street Journal*. He died in 2014. They reared their son, Angelo Grant Henderson, to show compassion toward others and to be an independent thinker. Her late husband was and still is widely admired and beloved by people in his adopted hometown of Detroit as well as by journalists and religious leaders across the country. Henderson said,

"It's never easy when a loved one dies suddenly. I really had to lean on my faith and trust God. He was in control, and I learned to accept that. Many days were extremely difficult, but I had a solid group of friends and colleagues who lifted me up."

As a working mother, Henderson admitted that she was extremely blessed to be in a position to negotiate her work hours with her supervisors, with a hard cut off at 5:30 p.m. in the office. But her work never ended at 5:30 p.m., especially as her job became a twenty-four-hour news operation, and her tasks and duties multiplied. She and her husband worked fifty-plus hours a week. It was her village of friends who were their saving grace on those days when breaking news prevented them from leaving the office. "There were at least six names on the school pickup authorization form [for my son]."

In 1999, the *Detroit Free Press* came calling for her at a time when new management was hired at the *Detroit News* and the environment changed. Henderson took another leap of faith. She worked for the *Free Press* as an assistant features editor and loved everything about the job—the people, the collective brainstorming, and the encouraging atmosphere. Nearly two years later, she was recruited to return to the *Detroit News*.

The *Free Press* did everything to convince her to stay, including have top editors and corporate executives call her at home. Ultimately, she decided to accept the position at the *Detroit News* because she saw it as a good career move. At the *News*, she would be working under a person that she knew and trusted, and intuitively felt that the move would take her career to the next level, and it did. She was features editor (2001-2007) and then became assistant managing editor (2007-2019).

When asked what she is most proud of about her career, Henderson pauses before responding. "Because of my ability to organize, connect with, and motivate staff, the executive editor tapped me to co-lead the largest change initiative at *The Detroit News* in 2009. That work inspired me to get a master's degree in organization development to help other organizations undergoing tremendous change."

After thirty-five years in the newsroom, Henderson's career has come full circle. She now is director of Cultural Competency at the

Felecia Henderson

Felecia Henderson with a Detroit News colleague in 2018.

Maynard Institute for Journalism Education, which gave her the tools to be successful in journalism. As an employee engagement specialist, she primarily serves as a liaison between the Maynard Institute and the Knight-Lenfest Table Stakes newsroom innovation program, training journalists in 100-plus print and broadcast newsrooms across the country on increasing diversity, equity, trust and inclusion in journalism.

What would she pass on to a budding journalist of color? "Don't be afraid to speak up. We are in the newsroom for two purposes: to excel at the job and ensure communities of color are accurately reflected in coverage."

Sadeqa Johnson is an international best-selling author of four novels, including Yellow Wife, *her most recent work. Her accolades include being the recipient of the National Book Club Award, the Phillis Wheatley Award, and the USA Best Book Award for best fiction. She lives near Richmond, Virginia.*

Chapter 15

Diane Graham Walker

Reporting Truth to Realize Power—Dedicated Consumer Advocate Reaps Results

As a veteran consumer and investigative reporter and television anchorwoman, Diane Graham Walker has advocated for those without a voice.

Walker has helped consumers form truces with slumlords, shady car dealers, and elusive insurance companies. She has comforted grieving mothers who have lost their sons and daughters to violence. And she has faced down menacing police in the middle of the night, all part of the hundreds of news stories she covered for her NBC-12 Richmond, Virginia, audiences before retiring in July 2021.

But on May 23, 2005, the tables turned. Walker's youngest brother, Billy Graham, was gunned down during an early morning jog near one of Richmond's public housing communities. *She* was now the person she normally interviewed.

Walker heard about the shooting from a family friend as she worked in her backyard. It took a moment before it all registered.

"I said, hold on, I have to finish this first," she said. "That was my way of processing." Although devastated and distraught in the weeks following her brother's murder, Walker transitioned from grieving sister to reporter as her journalistic instincts kicked into high gear. After the culprit was arrested, a mistake during preliminary hearings allowed him to return to the streets.

"So, he was in the wind," Walker recalled. But not for long.

"I used my platform to get people to call in and give information. We reached out and featured three or four unsolved murders and talked to families about their grief. We asked people to step up and say something. The Richmond Police Department ended up solving Billy's case." His killer surrendered to police June 17, 2005, following an intense manhunt and police pressure. RPD threatened to arrest the shooter's family members if they failed to cooperate with the investigation. The gunman gave himself up.

Billy Graham's killer stood trial, was convicted and sentenced. After serving fifteen years in prison, he was released in November 2019. And while Walker experienced "a strange feeling of anxiety" since his release, it didn't stop her from working to eradicate crime and senseless murder in Richmond and other communities before she retired.

After all, Richmond is home.

Walker grew up not far from where her brother was murdered in Richmond's Church Hill community. Located in the East End, it is a mix of elegant, historical homes, restaurants and businesses. St. John's

Diane Walker shown with WWBT (NBC12) colleagues in the early 1980s.

Church—Richmond's oldest church built in 1741, is within walking distance of where Walker grew up at East Broad Street and later on North Thirty-Fifth Street. Several African American churches anchor the community, hence its name. In recent years, much attention has been paid to Church Hill's nearby Shockoe Bottom area, which once was the second largest slave market in the United States.

Church Hill also is home to several public housing complexes, mainly occupied by African Americans. Residents of those communities often contacted Walker for help at NBC-12. She was happy to respond: whether it was motivating area businesses to rebuild and repair their homes, or helping to make Christmas a little better for struggling families, the elderly, and disabled. Walker also mentors high school and college students who want to become journalists, and her work repeatedly helped NBC-12 win the Associated Press award for Best News Operation of the Year. Walker's other honors include the Distinguished Consumer Service award from the Virginia Citizens Consumer Council and she was inducted into the Virginia Communications Hall of Fame in 2015.

More recently, Walker received the inaugural Community Champion Award from the leaders of Virginia Commonwealth University Health

Hume-Lee Transplant Center, and in April 2021, she was inducted into the National Academy of Television Arts and Sciences Gold and Silver Circle.

The second youngest of six children, Walker assumed many responsibilities in her two-parent, working-class household. Neither of her parents—Leroy Graham, a construction worker, or Mary Lee Graham—a domestic worker, graduated high school. Because her parents stayed busy working to support their family, Mary Graham instructed her children to write down any of their questions, and she would respond to the most urgent ones. It was then that Walker discovered the power of words, and she made sure that her questions always stood out.

Although her life started "with a lot of challenges," Walker never felt them while growing up. Her parents purchased their home in Church Hill with her construction worker father doing most of the repair work. (They later purchased several additional properties and a boat on which the family created many lasting memories on the water.) Despite her parents' strong work ethic, family time was important and included trips to the beach or drives to South Carolina during the summer.

But that process of writing down questions and waiting for the answers stayed with her and lit the spark for a career in journalism.

"I loved storytelling and reading and always wanted to do something with writing. I can remember using my hairbrush as a microphone. My brother would always tease me about it."

It was that same brother, Billy, who alerted Walker to a Black woman reporter he spotted on television in the early 1970s.

"Billy was downstairs when Bernie came on," said Walker, referring to Bernadine Simmons, then a reporter for the same NBC affiliate in Richmond where Walker eventually would work. "He screamed, 'There's a woman downstairs on TV who looks like you, and she's reporting the news!'" Walker knew then that her dream of becoming a broadcast journalist was possible, but it would not come without challenges. High school was somewhat of a blur because her mother was sick. It was a lengthy illness and required that Walker balance school and her duties at home, which included caring for her mother.

"She was sick for a long time, and I took care of her," said Walker. "My mother had done so much for me and instilled in me the need to take care of family."

But a close relationship with her English teacher continued to encourage her love of writing and journalism. "Ms. Bettis helped shape me into taking challenges and setbacks and using your power from within to change and improve things for yourself."

After her mother's death, Walker turned her attention to college upon graduating from Armstrong High School. An astute Armstrong guidance counselor knew that the University of Virginia was seeking students of Walker's caliber and potential; financial assistance was hers for the asking.

Walker started her first year at UVA still mourning the loss of her mother. Yet, she believes that her mother's strong spiritual faith and her parents' high regard for education further motivated her.

"That's the type of person she was," Walker said of her mother, who believed in gathering information to make the best decisions. "I tried not to be absorbed in the whole sadness of her death, and UVA made it easier." Like many elite, predominantly white American universities during the 1970s, UVA sought to enroll more Black students following the civil rights movement of the 1960s and growing calls for admitting racial minorities as well as women. A 1969 lawsuit forced UVA to open its undergraduate school to women, a plan that initially was to be implemented over ten years. However, full coeducation occurred in 1972. Walker entered UVA in 1974, just two years later.

As a speech communications and English major, Walker worked hard toward becoming a broadcast journalist. After graduating in 1978, she had no industry connections like some of her classmates and peers, so she took a job back home in Virginia Union University's President's Office writing and editing communications, which included alumni publications, coming out of that office. While the job was fun and she learned a lot, it wasn't her dream job. She sent her resume to Richmond's three commercial television stations and eventually got a call from NBC-12's news director Ron Miller.

"Ron believed in my potential and pushed for me to be hired. It also was an era of affirmative action and television stations had to adhere to FCC [Federal Communications Commission] guidelines. It leveled the field for many of us who were starting out." Although it was several months before things opened up at what Richmonders know as "Channel 12," Miller suggested that Walker take a position in sales. She worked in sales for nearly a year before switching to news. "I started in 1980 as a general assignment reporter, then city council and weekend anchor. I enjoyed that level of politics. Then I covered courts for a while, but it required a lot of sitting. I enjoyed being on the street and meeting people."

NBC-12's slogans "12 On Your Side," and "Call 12" could well have been created with Walker's consumer and investigative reporting skills in mind. Her pivot in 1994 from City of Richmond beat reporting to helping viewers navigate complex business-related issues was a "natural evolution," because, along with providing resources and guidance to viewers, she enjoyed helping them resolve or find solutions to problems. Walker's career continued to evolve that year at NBC-12 when the station and Fox Richmond entered a partnership which resulted in Fox News at 10's September 1994 debut as the area's only prime-time newscast. And Walker was in the anchor seat.

"It proved to be a lucrative partnership," she said, adding that 1994 "is also when I moved into my '12 On Your Side' consumer-investigative role, which was a natural transition. The work was more like a ministry than just reporting."

Walker is proud to have helped "Call 12," a popular programming feature that began in the 1980s, resolve consumer problems, filter possible news stories and achieve diversity among the on-air volunteers who handled calls from the public.

She believed that the people who answered the help lines should reflect the population that the station served. Walker spent several weeks reaching out and promoting "12 On Your Side" to Black sororities, fraternities, churches and retirees. It took a while but it worked.

"My mission was to change the face of it, making it more inclusive and user friendly for people of all races. I'm happy I was able to do that."

Despite her popularity and ability to walk into spaces where she is warmly greeted, Walker has experienced several incidents of racial discord. During a telephone conversation, a white woman once told her that she did not want a Black person in her home, unaware that Walker was Black. "She apologized when I told her that the color green killed her son, not a Black person," said Walker. And she has been stopped several times by Chesterfield County police for minor infractions. One situation was so bad that she ended up calling the police on the police.

"I was pulled over for allegedly running a red light," she recalled. "I was so afraid to get out of the car because the officer was screaming at me and trying to open my door. I called 911 and requested a supervisor to come to the scene. The supervisor arrived, apologized, said the officer was new and overzealous and told me I could leave.

Other harassing incidents involving police followed.

"I'm not sure why Chesterfield police started stopping me. Sometimes I would get pulled over two and three times a week years ago. Maybe it had something to do with a story I covered where my photographer and I stood our ground about having a legal right to stay where we were standing. At one point, my news director at the time considered giving me a hidden camera to record those frightening encounters. I just endured them. On one occasion, a police officer walked up to me in a convenience store and quietly told me 'I'm sorry.' He went on to say officers would meet to talk about stopping me and harassing me. I was speechless."

In another incident, Walker's social media post stirred up trolls who were intent on spreading untruths. It took a tsunami of support to stop the wave of hate.

In 2015, Walker posted a blurb on her Facebook page about a feel-good story of a police officer who spontaneously took time out to play a game of catch with children. In her remarks, Walker noted that police

After a nearly four-decade career in television, Diane Walker retired from Richmond, Virginia's NBC-12 in 2021.

officers in some parts of the country have gotten a lot of criticism, "some of it deserved," then went on to say, "But, here's one instance we should see more of: a cop who stops to play catch with some neighborhood kids."

Walker wrote that the kids' mom "feared the worst when that officer first got out of his cruiser and was headed toward them." But the end result, Walker said, was a "heartwarming story" that she encouraged her followers to tune in for more later than afternoon.

While it was an overall positive story, some police supporters took offense with her characterization of what happened and created social media pages that maligned Walker and demanded that she apologize and be fired. Walker initially refused to apologize, but eventually did so a few days later. What strengthened her "was over the course of twenty-four hours, people all over the world" stood up for her. And she kept her job.

Walker now regrets the apology, particularly in the wake of George Floyd, a Black man who was choked to death on May 25, 2020, by Derek Chauvin, a white Minneapolis police officer who kept his knee on Floyd's neck.

"I feel ahead of my time—here we are now in 2020 calling for police reform."

Through the years, Walker often received offers to work for other news stations, but she never entertained them due to family dynamics.

"Broadcast journalism is tough on any marriage, it's not a nine-to-five job, and even before social media there were long hours and being subject to be called back in. It's hard. You do what you can to balance, but you always feel as if you're letting someone down. So, you do your best and give God the rest. And you eventually get to the point where you stop comparing yourself to other people who may not be going through the same struggles."

A divorced mother of two children, Rhoni Jae and Allyn, Walker also is a grandmother who enjoys spending time with her granddaughter. Walker retired on July 16, 2021, from the news station that she had called home for four decades. She enjoyed her work, but she knows that there is more to life than just work. She learned part of that lesson when her brother Billy died. Now she has moved on to her next "story." While she may miss being the one in the anchor seat or behind the microphone, she is comfortable knowing the role she played and the work she was able to do for so many others.

"I gave them a voice when they didn't have one. That's what journalism is all about."

Chapter 16

Sonya Ross

Cultivating Sources Others Ignored—From Covering the White House to Becoming Unmuted

By Tammie Smith

In 1995, Associated Press journalist Sonya Ross was assigned to cover the White House and all the trappings of power the beat demands. Bill Clinton was president, followed by George W. Bush, who was elected in 2000. Ross, who by then had worked for the Associated Press for twenty-seven years, discovered that the prime position many journalists aspire to daily as being fairly routine. Anytime the president traveled, the Associated Press sent two reporters along. Ross rotated those trips with other AP reporters.

"It was such an amazing thing. You are allegedly the cream of the crop, but you do so much work that is not grand at all. You are herded around like cattle. Or you were at that time," Ross said.

Much of that changed on September 11, 2001. Ross was the AP reporter in the press pool that had traveled with President Bush to Sarasota, Florida, to visit an elementary school to promote his administration's No Child Left Behind education reform initiative. Word made its way to the president's people about the first plane crashing into World Trade Center North Tower, but everyone assumed it was just a tragic accident. Subsequent plane crashes into the South Tower and the Pentagon shifted everything into overdrive.

Rushed back to Air Force One, Ross still remembers having no idea where they were headed when they flew to an Air Force base near Shreveport, Louisiana. Later, a pared-down reporting pool reboarded Air Force One. Ross learned later she was part of the bunker pool—the group of reporters that accompany a president being evacuated out of harm's way.

"Quiet as it's kept, the press pool traveling with Bush that day was quite diverse. I wanted desperately to get a piece of the story, as big a piece as locked-down conditions permitted," Ross said.

"I had so many thoughts in my head. Would they really tell us if we land in Canada or Mexico? Because that would mean Bush abdicated power."

She also thought of her own mortality.

"If this plane went down right now, my life would get explained away as one of the 2,750 others who perished. And nobody would care. I prayed a lot. And I sent an email asking people who tried reaching me that way to pray for our country."

By the time the day ended, and in the immediate days after, America learned that nineteen militants associated with the Islamic extremist group al Qaeda had hijacked four airplanes in the United States. Two of the planes were flown into the Twin Towers of the World Trade Center in New York City, a third plane hit the Pentagon just outside Washington,

D.C., and the fourth plane crashed in a field in Shanksville, Pennsylvania. In addition to the 2,750 people killed, hundreds more were injured during what has become known as the 9/11 terrorist attacks.

Ross, as one of small group of Black journalists who have held the coveted position of White House correspondent, recalled, "It's almost as if the years were just a blur."

While her time spent as a White House correspondent was a highlight of those years, covering the White House was not on Ross's agenda when she took her first position with the news service in 1986 as an intern with the AP bureau in Atlanta, her hometown. Working for the news service harkened back to the journalistic tendencies Ross displayed as a child.

"I had a cassette recorder and would tape a report every day about things going on in my little world," she said. "I kept a diary. My mom had us writing letters to our grandfather every summer. We subscribed to three newspapers—the *Atlanta Constitution*, the *Atlanta Daily World*, and the *Atlanta Voice*—plus *Ebony* and *Jet* magazines. A voracious reader, Ross's father placed the newspapers in her hands when he "got tired of signing library permission slips for me to check out books considered too mature for my age. When I began to develop a cursing habit, he gave me a dictionary and told me, 'There are much better words to tell people off with in here.' In short order, I got into a fight at school for calling a mean girl a 'cretin.'"

Later, after enrolling at the University of Georgia in Athens to study biology, Ross soon decided that science was not for her. She confided in her sister's father, Harmon Perry, a photojournalist for the *Daily World* and a bureau chief for Johnson Publications, that she was considering becoming a journalist because she wanted to help change the "unfair" way in which the media portrayed Black people. "He said, 'OK. Just know Black folks ain't gonna appreciate ya.'"

Perry's advice failed to discourage Ross who switched to pre-journalism during her sophomore year, followed by public relations, speech communications, and ultimately Black studies.

She ended up leaving school after her third year, in 1983, when she ran out of money and financial aid dried up. Back home, she got a job at a local department store to build savings to return to school. But instead of going back to Athens, she stayed in Atlanta and enrolled in Georgia State University. At the time, the school did not have an African American studies undergraduate major, but it did have a journalism program. She shaped her Black studies courses into a minor and majored in journalism.

"I had a racial emphasis on my professional pursuits from the beginning," Ross said.

She took classes during the day and in the evenings worked in the "morgue," or archives, at the *Atlanta Journal-Constitution*. She applied for an internship at the paper but was not selected. Later, during an ASNE Minorities in the Newsroom job fair, she met Lamar Matthews, an AP assistant bureau chief who was recruiting students for internship positions. He looked over her resume and one bylined story and told her point-blank that she needed to write more stories.

"After that, every time I wrote an article for the student paper at Georgia State I would walk it to the AP bureau, which was just on the other end of Marietta Street," Ross recalled.

Her efforts and persistence paid off. Matthews called her the next spring to come in to take the internship test. In a noisy room with a manual typewriter, she spent two hours editing sample stories, compiling a story from a set of facts, writing copy for print and broadcast, taking a vocabulary quiz, and editing sentences. Three weeks later Matthews called and offered her the internship. Successful completion of the internship meant she would be offered a job.

"I would leave there just completely drained of energy every single day because the work was so hard-charging and aggressive," she recalled. "But I was excited about what I was learning and doing. I was being trusted with real assignments. I felt this real responsibility to be accurate and sharp."

Her internship was extended two weeks so that she could help with covering a local, high-profile election—the 1986 race between civil rights icons John Lewis and Julian Bond for a congressional seat. Lewis won. The next spring, during her final semester at Georgia State, the AP asked Ross whether she could start sooner than planned. In May 1987, she began working as a general assignment reporter with the AP bureau in Atlanta.

"When I walked into the AP in Atlanta, Georgia, as Black as Atlanta was, I was the only Black reporter they had, and I was the only Black person in that office," Ross said.

It was a good time to be covering news in Atlanta. There was a lot going on in the city nicknamed "Hotlanta" and often touted as a mecca for Black politics, business, and entertainment. As the new reporter, Ross worked nights and weekends, covering cops and mainly rewriting stories picked up from local member papers. On her days off, she began to experience her hometown in new ways.

"I think what made a difference for me was the flow of the news at that time. I could see there was so much major Black news happening in that town that I felt the nation would care about. So I began to chase that news. I found myself getting news that white people didn't know about. Or didn't care about. That very much played into the reason that I had selected journalism in the first place."

At the AP, she earned a reputation for being able to cultivate sources who could tell her what was going on behind the scenes.

"I think they thought there was some magical formula I was using to get these stories. I was just Black and curious," Ross said.

Her editors said she had a "natural ear for the political." Big stories she followed include Maynard Jackson Jr.'s campaign for a third term as Atlanta mayor and Andrew Young's failed bid to become governor of Georgia.

She also spent time covering the state General Assembly, but by 1992, she was ready for a change. There was an opening in the AP Washington, D.C., bureau for an arts and entertainment reporter. She applied and waited.

In the meantime, in Los Angeles, the Rodney King verdict came down and protests erupted. In March 1991, King, a construction worker, was violently beaten by Los Angeles police officers during his arrest for fleeing and resisting arrest. A civilian recorded the beating and sent it to a local news station. The four officers were tried on charges of police brutality; three were acquitted, and the jury failed to reach a verdict on one charge for the fourth. Within hours of the acquittals, the 1992 Los Angeles riots started.

It was all hands on deck for the AP. Ross said her supervisors asked her to pack a bag in case she needed to go to Los Angeles. But there was news to cover at home when students at the Atlanta University Center began to protest the verdict.

"I was about the only thing they could send in there because I was young enough to blend in with the students and really see what was happening," she said. She was on the street for about twelve hours straight reporting that story.

Not long after, Jon Wolfman, the AP bureau chief in Washington, D.C., invited her up for an interview. When she got there, she learned it was not for the arts beat. He wanted to create an urban affairs beat covering race and cities, and he wanted her for that job.

"I told him that urban affairs is fine, but really the problem in America was racial. I felt I might as well be honest. The problem is more racial than urban," Ross recalled.

She moved to Washington in June 1992, taking on a new beat covering civil rights and urban affairs. She covered the Congressional Black Caucus, activist C. Delores Tucker's push against gangsta rap, the NAACP, and other race-related topics. Her work was noticed. In 1995, she was promoted to cover the White House.

When Ross left the White House beat in 2002, she became an editor in the AP's world services division, supervising a team of four reporters covering the nation's capital for an international audience, and writing news analysis. When the foreign affairs news editor left, she took on some of those duties, hoping it would prove she was a team player and ready for more responsibility and a higher-profile leadership role.

"I was doing two jobs, plus writing news analysis at the beginning of the war in Afghanistan. While juggling way too much work, not getting paid for that extra job that I had been given, I am thinking 'is it really necessary to do all of this to show that I can do this?' There just seemed to be a constant 'prove yourself.' I'm saying this about the industry, not just the AP."

In 2004, she became a regional news editor, regarding that position as a stepping-stone to higher management as she had seen others do. Two years later, she asked, *What's next?* She had turned down AP's offer of a position in Johannesburg, not wanting to leave her mother, who was getting older, stateside. Later, she applied for a job as assistant bureau chief in Washington. It was not lost on her that an AP reporter, who had covered the White House alongside her and was on a similar career track, was now a bureau chief.

"I was still trying to get an opportunity to move up from news editor."

She was turned down for the job.

"I said this is racial. There is no reason for me to have been passed over for that job. I could languish another six years or try to find a career path for myself. Industry conditions by that time were terrible. There weren't many jobs available. News organizations were furloughing employees and (there were) buyouts."

She considered leaving journalism but Barack Obama's election as president stopped her.

Ross proposed to management that they broaden race and ethnicity coverage to chronicle the transformation of the United States into a multicultural society.

After two years of negotiations, the AP in 2010 named her race and ethnicity editor.

"There was no staff, no budget, no real authority to do anything. I should have been given direct reports right off the bat, not 'you can borrow this reporter or that reporter,' or having to call around the AP begging for reporters. I should have been given budget authority. The ability to spend money or for them to say here is how much your journalism effort gets in the overall AP budget. More importantly, I expected to get buy-in from the top so that when I went about doing my work I wouldn't get the brush off from my colleagues. They gave me nothing."

As those negotiations were underway, so was an internal discrimination complaint she had filed against the AP for how she was treated as an applicant for the assistant bureau chief position.

That episode wasn't her first brush with bigotry. During her first job at the AP years earlier, the newsroom discussions sometimes touched on racially sensitive topics, and she found herself on the defensive.

One such discussion was about affirmative action. The AP internship she completed was an initiative to increase minorities and women in the newsroom. Ross told her coworkers that, yes, she got in the door because of affirmative action, but her skills were keeping her there.

"That experience gave me sort of a brutal honesty that I never shed. I said I have a responsibility to be frank with these folks especially if they are going to be frank with me. I would be sugarcoating it if I ever said it was easy. It was not. It was very difficult." The internal investigation conducted by HR ruled in favor of the AP on the discrimination complaint. Ross said the work situation became even more hostile. In 2012, she filed a federal complaint Labor Department's Office of Federal Contract Compliance Programs accusing the AP of retaliating against her.

"I had to do something to protect the career I had built," she said.

"I didn't see any value in being silent at that point. I felt I had absolutely nothing to lose. And I couldn't let AP just unceremoniously shove me out the door. I really never understood where the hostility came from. I never knew where it came from. Why all of a sudden they were so hostile to me when all I had ever done was work hard for the AP, do the best I could, and make them look good. There were people in the industry who very much admired the work I was doing."

For most of her career, she had praised the AP as flexible and offering opportunities. When her career hit a brick ceiling, the only difference between her and others on the same career trajectory seemed to be race.

The Labor Department's investigation took four years and the Office of Federal Contract Compliance Program issued a finding of retaliation and granted me a right to sue. She had ninety days to take legal action.

She sued the AP in May 2016. Outwardly, she appeared to have it all together. Inside she was in turmoil. She turned to her sister, a minister, for spiritual counseling. On one trip to New York City to meet with AP brass, she recalled finding a quiet corner in a train station to call her sister for strength. They prayed together.

The suit was settled in 2019, and Ross retired from the news service.

"I had been batting AP for nearly a decade. By 2019, I was really more than a decade in trying to move up. I gave up trying to move up and just said I am going to survive. I am going to outlast the bigotry," Ross said.

"I feel good that when I had a chance to take a stand I took it," she said.

In 2019, she co-founded Black Women Unmuted, a news and media website that covers underreported news about the political engagement of Black women. Despite what she endured, she still encourages young African Americans to pursue journalism and she is proud of the journalists she has mentored.

"They have every right to do this job," said Ross. "They should never ever let the fear, mistreatment by white people, keep them from chasing their dream if this is it. They have every right to do this career."

Tammie Smith spent nearly forty years as a business, health, and general assignment reporter for the Richmond Times-Dispatch, the Tennessean, and the New Journal and Guide newspapers. She lives in Richmond, Virginia.

Chapter 17

Teresa J. Styles

Blending Black Voices into the "Way It Was" at *CBS News*—
Broadcast Pioneer's Pivotal Lessons for Students

In 1980 when former Massachusetts Senator Ted Kennedy sought the Democratic nomination for president against Jimmy Carter, he stumbled during an interview when asked why he wanted to be president of the world's foremost superpower. When the hour-long interview aired on CBS on November 4, it destroyed Kennedy's chances of getting the nod. Carter defeated him in the primary, and Kennedy never ran for president again.

The broadcast earned a prestigious Peabody Award, and among those who contributed to the documentary was an African American female journalist named Teresa Styles.

Throughout her illustrious journalism career, Styles contributed to many groundbreaking and award-winning documentaries and news stories on the network level. Yet, she considers the "Blacks in America" assignment, a 1979 piece that helped end segregated medical practices in states such as Mississippi that were accepting Medicaid funds, her greatest legacy. Part one of *Blacks in America* on *CBS Reports* examined race relations in Mississippi following the 1954 historic *Brown v. Topeka (Kansas) Board of Education* decision.

For the series, Ed Bradley, the late and highly revered CBS reporter and *60 Minutes* correspondent, interviewed students and teachers at the integrated Tupelo High School and at a segregated, all-white academy in Lexington, Mississippi. He questioned Black teachers in an all-Black high school and visited the waiting room of a segregated doctor's office. The documentary also captured footage of a boycott in Lexington to protest Black unemployment and the mayor's response, as well as a Ku Klux Klan counter demonstration in Tupelo.

As the associate producer, Styles pulled together much of the report's content, which received the Alfred I. DuPont–Columbia University Award in 1980. Before heading to Mississippi, she spent months reading newspapers, magazines from the CBS news center library, known as the "morgue," and copy from Associated Press, Reuters, and United Press International news wires and conducting telephone interviews. Part two of "Blacks in America" filmed in Philadelphia focused on the volatile racial issues in that city at that time.

"In those days, we didn't have today's fast-paced technology," Styles said. "It was also before the satellite was widely used. If you wanted footage from overseas, you had to have it flown [to the United States]."

Once the research was complete, the team headed to their destinations. They also spent time in Chicago developing the documentary. "Although many cities were considered, we focused on Mississippi and were there for months. We're looking for stories up and down the streets in little towns and at (Ku Klux) Klan rallies," she said, adding that Black residents in many of the small towns sought them out to share their stories of hardship in the segregated South.

Styles recalled how she and Bradley were stopped, frisked, and harassed by police on the interstate when returning from a Klan rally in Tupelo to pursue their coverage in Tchula, Mississippi. Undeterred, they continued their work.

"When you would hope there would have been progress, the same type of segregation in schools was still happening," Styles said. "Segregated Black schools did not have proper supplies and were using second-rate textbooks. White schools had it better, along with the academies and private schools."

Styles was further dismayed after entering a white doctor's office to discover segregated waiting rooms, in direct violation of the federal civil rights law passed some sixteen years earlier in 1964. Waiting rooms for white patients were light and cheery, whereas such spaces were dark and unwelcoming for Black patients. CBS reported its findings to the U.S. Department of Justice before the documentary aired, and the doctor was ordered to desegregate the facility.

Styles's innate curiosity, thirst for learning and attention to civil and human rights were honed in her hometown of Atlanta where it was not uncommon for her to walk past the homes of the Rev. Dr. Martin Luther King, Jr. and other civil rights activists to and from school.

Atlanta has long been a place for Black progress. As a result, her parents Julian and Jennie Styles were active in the community. A Black officer in the Army during World War II and a federal employee her father attended Clark College and her mother taught as a reading specialist. They stressed the importance of education and steered all four of their children—Gwenelle, Teresa, Julian, and Marty—to seek degrees from historically Black colleges and universities such as Clark, Spelman, and Virginia State, as well as advanced degrees from Columbia, New York University, Northwestern, and the University of North Carolina at Chapel Hill. They have all had extensive and notable careers in academia, journalism, and government, she said.

Her love for film began with her parents when they made attending the segregated film theaters a ritual on weekends. During the week, she attended Henry McNeal Turner High School, named after a minister, politician, and the twelfth elected and consecrated bishop of the African Methodist Episcopal Church. It was considered one of Atlanta's most prestigious high schools for Black students. After graduating, Styles enrolled at Spelman College in Atlanta, one of only two all-women's HBCUs in the country, and majored in English. A trained pianist and upright bass violin player, she also dabbled in theater while there.

Styles graduated from Spelman in 1972 and enrolled at Northwestern University in Evanston, Illinois, to pursue a master's degree in film criticism. She also worked as a news researcher at Chicago's *CBS* TV affiliate, WBBM, where she mainly researched how the station could comply with the Federal Communications Commission's (FCC) rules and regulations.

After earning her master's degree and graduating from Northwestern in 1973, Styles returned to her hometown and worked at WETV (now known as PBA Atlanta) as a production assistant, using her skills in filming and editing from graduate school.

"It was when we used film, not video, for news. I also honed my skills as a technical director in the control room," she explained.

Her interest and work on the WETV locally produced show *Cinema Showcase,* allowed her to work with Kirk Douglas and Robert Mitchum, huge Hollywood stars at the time. Not only did she interview Douglas and Mitchum, but she also spent a day with legendary comedian, actress, and TV star Lucille Ball.

Although she was back in Atlanta, Styles kept in touch with CBS employees and executives, including Robert J. Wussler, who had hired her in Chicago when she worked for CBS's affiliate WBBM. Wussler became a senior executive for CBS' news and sports divisions, president of the CBS Television Network in the 1970s and later the top aide to cable TV pioneer Ted Turner during the expansion of Turner's cable TV operations. Also in Styles's Rolodex was Joan Schneider, who was instrumental in helping her get hired at CBS in New York when the network had to follow federal mandates to hire women and minorities.

"Many women started in the executive secretarial pool," Styles said. "CBS founder William B. Paley made it his mission to know the new hires by placing them in all the various divisions to determine their skills. It was Paley's way of moving us into journalism jobs—for women and minorities. This was part of a federal mandate for broadcasters.

"New hires worked in censorship, music, news, sales, and after working in every department, many landed in the *CBS* News division's research department," she continued. "Becoming a member of the research team was the stepping-stone to producing, which entailed any story that a correspondent was trying to do for all the news programs including *60 Minutes* or *CBS Reports*. Researchers did a lot of fact-checking, some location work and helped develop questions. This was the model for most news organizations that were hiring men and women during that time."

Styles worked as a researcher until 1979, when she became an associate producer. One of her last segments appeared on *CBS News Sunday Morning*, hosted by the network's legendary broadcaster and storyteller Charles Kuralt. Styles said she helped conceive the show while aboard flights from Washington, D.C., to Topeka, Kansas, in preparation for the "Blacks in America" story. She still has the notes she wrote regarding the show, and recalls the main idea being the need for a show that could compete with religious programs being produced by networks.

"My main idea was the need for something serene and tranquil, which really ended up being those ending photos of wonderful scenic landscapes and mountains," she recalled.

"The president of news at that time was Bill Leonard, who'd helped create *60 Minutes*. Leonard called the executive producer Robert Northshield while the team was in Washington, D.C., and asked him to develop a new Sunday show," she recalled. "So, from D.C. to Topeka, some of my ideas came to fruition. I had a lot to do with the first concept."

Amid traditional news networks' concerns over growing cable competition, whispers about mergers and falling profits, Styles saw the proverbial writing on the wall and left *CBS* and New York in 1985. She returned south to join Savannah State College in Georgia as an assistant professor. She described Savannah as "a beautiful city and the opposite of the fast-paced New York." Being at Savannah State and eventually other HBCUs, allowed Styles to give back and contribute to her culture all that she had learned at *CBS*.

In 1990 she accepted a position as an assistant professor in Bennett College's mass communications program. Located in Greensboro, North Carolina, Bennett, is the country's only other all-women's HBCU. At Bennett, Styles helped develop the mass communications program, and became the director of the college's Women's Studies Program. In that capacity, she developed and implemented a seminar series, Maya Angelou and Friends, featuring the late poet Dr. Maya Angelou. The seminars were titled "Dr. Maya Angelou: Sisterhood," "AIDS Education," (April 1991) and "A Conversation With A South African Writer, Loretta Ncogobo" (November 1992).

"The final content of the three seminars was completed at the home of Dr. Angelou over a wonderful meal when she [Angelou] served as a professor at Wake Forest University," Styles said fondly.

Noted writer-in-residence Mari Evans was also at Bennett at that time, and their collaborative work resulted in Styles's working on Evans's production and panel of Zora Neal Hurston's *Their Eyes Were Watching God* at Purdue/Indiana University in October 1995.

All the while, Styles continued to work in television, producing documentaries for UNC-TV public broadcasting in North Carolina.

After three years at Bennett, Styles joined the faculty and staff at nearby North Carolina Agricultural and Technical State University in 1993. At A&T, Styles rapidly climbed the ranks in the Department of Journalism and Mass Communication, becoming tenured in 1999 after earning her PhD in mass communication a year earlier from the University of North Carolina at Chapel Hill.

By then, Styles had served as the journalism department's chair from 2003 to 2006 and had successfully led the department in obtaining full accreditation for the unit from the Accrediting Council on Education in Journalism and Mass Communication. The only other institution in

North Carolina to receive such accreditation at that time was UNC-Chapel Hill, from which she had earned her PhD.

In 2015 Styles retired from A&T as a full professor. She had received numerous awards and honors, including the UNC Board of Governors Award for Teaching Excellence and the Willie Parker Peace History Book Award by the North Carolina Society of Historians. She is an author of *Mens et Manus: A Pictorial History of North Carolina Agricultural & Technical State University*, which celebrates A&T's 125 years. The book was released in 2015.

Styles's entry into academia was a natural segue for journalists like her who witnessed and documented many of the news media's most revolutionary moments in history, culture and politics. Ever the documentarian, historian and journalism educator, Styles, who became an adjunct professor at Morehouse College in Atlanta after retiring from A&T, reflected on contemporary journalism's origins.

"Many of the first newspapers served a partisan cause and they still do," she said. "However, during the 1950s through the 1970s, media criticism prompted news organizations and journalism schools to develop standards that would ensure accurate, balanced and fair reporting. A lot of it came at a time when students like me were coming out of college. We were appalled at the trauma created during the Nixon years that the crusade for accurate reporting became a mainstay. This is an unfortunate time we currently live in where all the standards are challenged."

Today, progress is more visible in some of the nation's newsrooms, despite the fact that many print newspapers have been downsized, involved in mergers or folded. Yet, in 2021 alone, Black women have attained executive news leadership roles at MSNBC, *ABC News*, the *Dallas Morning News*, the *Houston Chronicle*, the *Charlotte Observer*, and the *Miami Herald*.

Styles, a stalwart news consumer, is heartened by the newsroom's recent advances.

"I think it is interesting, refreshing and wonderful to know that we have several African American women in executive positions. In my day, we were pleased to be the first to work in any type of position," she said. To become an executive producer was an extraordinary feat."

Sadly, such changes only emerged following a decade of social unrest and a renewed awareness in 2020 about the mistreatment African Americans have long suffered, similar to the racial protests during the summer of 1967 that led to the Kerner Commission Report and ultimately women such as herself entering major network newsrooms.

Styles said she is fortunate to have reported stories "that had major impact on society and moved us to the greater good."

Yet, the work continues.

"Here it is fifty years later and we see some of the same stories as we did back then, all those documentaries—*The CIA's Secret Army*, *Teddy*, and *Blacks in America, What Shall We Do About Mother*—were an effort to bring an understanding of how to make the world better, which is so very elusive."

Despite journalism's fluctuations, Styles encouraged her students to continue pushing forward to make an impact. She also reminded them that if she could leave her hometown of Atlanta to work in New York City with some of the world's preeminent journalists, so could they.

"Don't let people tell you that you have to work local," she cautioned. "In broadcast, many of us started as secretaries, desk assistants and researchers with the ultimate goal being to produce. A producer has ideas based on what is going on in the world and what we all need to know in a fair and balanced way. It was exciting. I realized it was because I've always been curious and fascinated with telling the truth."

PART 4

Racing to the Top

Chapter 18

Pam McAllister Johnson

Ambition, Confidence, and a Rapid Ascent—Opportunity Knocked, Enabling Her to Be Called "First"

By Cathy Gant Hill

Pam McAllister Johnson crossed the threshold into posterity when she became the first African American woman publisher at the *Ithaca Journal*, a daily mainstream newspaper in Ithaca, New York, on December 10, 1982.

Yet, from her own experiences, coming of age during the civil rights era of the 1950s and 1960s and arriving in the workforce during affirmative action, Johnson encountered—and conquered—a host of racist, sexist, and elitist behavior:

- The Latina high school guidance counselor, who discouraged her from attending the University of Wisconsin–Madison, suggesting instead that she consider a historically Black college or university or a smaller college.

- A white college professor who, upon hearing Johnson affirm that she was interested in a television career, responded aloud that his friend, who taught such a course, would find it interesting "to have a little color" in his broadcast class. His class was all white.

- The white male news director at a commercial radio station, who pounded his fist on a table when he heard she had been hired and said he was not going to have any "GD woman working for him."

- The phone call she received as publisher from a woman who—ignorant of Johnson's race—wanted the paper to write an editorial because her neighborhood was being integrated, and she mistrusted African Americans, adding, "You know Black people smell."

- The *Ithaca Journal* reporter who brazenly told her at the publisher's welcoming party, "Pam, we have a good paper here, and you better not f—— it up."

In what would become a hallmark of her direct style and leadership approach, Johnson deftly handled each insult. She bested the guidance counselor by gaining admission to the University of Wisconsin, earning four degrees there, two of them doctoral—a joint Ph.D. in Mass Communication and Educational Psychology. Although perturbed at the college instructor's classroom comment "in front of God and everybody," she did not let him know it, choosing to take the TV class and doing so well that she ended up hosting her own Wisconsin Public Broadcasting news show. The recruiter who helped her get hired at the radio station made a point of telling the staff that Johnson had more credentials than many of them, and Johnson wore down the fist-pounder to the degree that they became and remained friends long after she'd moved on. Rather than choosing to "go off" on the racist caller, when she was publisher, Johnson listened and then politely directed her to an editor to let her respond to the outrageous request. The reporter at the party, she said, may have been neither racist nor sexist, just impertinent.

"If I had taken it personally, I would have fired him," Johnson said. "But I knew that he was proud about the paper, and I was proud that he was proud of the paper. When you don't like someone, you still have to work with him the next day. That's what I kept in mind. I had to focus on the next thing for the job. I also realize that you only have so much energy. You can use it to get back at someone, or you can use it to get ahead. Your choice."

Johnson had not intended to become a newspaper publisher. She had advanced degrees and work experience in journalism and intended to remain a crusading journalist. Yet, she had also majored in education. So, from 1979 to 1981, Johnson taught journalism courses at Norfolk State University in Virginia and had developed a reputation for preparing her students for interviews and to such an extent that Gannett executives took notice. Two of her former NSU students who achieved journalism distinction are Derek T. Dingle, executive vice president and chief content officer at *Black Enterprise* magazine, and Nathan McCall, a former *Washington Post* reporter, university professor and author of several books.

What she did at Norfolk State, she also did in microcosms when visiting other historically Black colleges and universities where she helped mentor and train student journalists.

Johnson further piqued Gannett's interest when she won fellowships from the American Newspaper Publishers Association and the American Press Institute. Her intelligence and ideas about the news industry eventually led Gannett executives to approach her about becoming a publisher for one of its properties. This was during a time when 61 percent of the United States' nearly 1,700 daily newspapers employed no minorities, and Black managers were rare. Gannett was serious about hiring and advancing journalists of color, so when the opportunity was offered, the energetic Johnson jumped at the chance.

Truth Tellers: *The Power and Presence of Black Women Journalists Since 1960*

Earlier in 1982, Johnson began learning her publisher's role as a general manager at the *Courier-News* in Bridgewater, New Jersey. Four short months later—in December 1982—she was catapulted into the president and publisher position at the *Ithaca Journal*, where she would oversee the directors of advertising, circulation, editorial, printing, personnel, and community relations. Johnson didn't believe that she was fully prepared, but she was confident, ambitious, and trusted that she would learn quickly what she needed to do. She outlined her goals, rolled up her sleeves, and went in.

She likes challenges, prepares relentlessly, is generous, and uses humor to help push past obstacles. Call her "Dr. McAllister Johnson" and she often responds, "Please, call me Pam." Johnson has barely slowed in more than fifty years to take stock of her noteworthy rankings, including first African American woman (and the tenth woman ever) to lead a daily newspaper.

As a star in the crown of Gannett, a behemoth media holder acquired by GateHouse Media in 2019, Johnson was on a first-name basis with Allen Neuharth, the revered and colorful Gannett executive and *USA Today* founder.

"As I said to Al [Neuharth], I always wanted to be a '10,' and this is probably the closest I'll ever be to a '10,'" Johnson recalled.

Neuharth laughed. "It's not a big deal that you can be the first Black woman publisher," he told her. "I'm looking forward to the day that we can fire Black executives and it won't be a big brouhaha."

While Johnson's ascension at Gannett was, in part, based on her gender and race, ultimately her success would be measured by her ability to transcend race while performing such a demanding job.

Still, Johnson did her part to maintain diversity in journalism, leading the *Ithaca Journal* for thirteen years. She left the newspaper in 1995.

"The job was twenty-four seven. As a publisher, you are never off," she said.

Johnson worked for a short time as an assistant to one of Gannett's regional vice presidents in nearby Binghamton. She left that position intending to retire, and she did for a while, mostly playing golf. Retirement in her 50s was too sedate a pace, and Johnson then headed to California to be the chief operating officer for Westworld Productions, a computer publishing company in Beverly Hills, California. In 2002, she was appointed as the R. M. Seaton Professional Journalism Endowed Faculty Chair at Kansas State University. A year later, Johnson was recruited as the director of the School of Journalism and Broadcasting at Western Kentucky University.

Johnson's ability to create lasting impressions and attract legions of fans was shaped years before she took the helm at the *Ithaca Journal*. She stood out from the pack, with television, radio, newspaper, and higher education experience. Johnson had internships at CBS affiliate stations in Chicago and Madison, Wisconsin. Her first post-college job was at the *Chicago Tribune* in 1967 where she and policeman-turned-journalist Joe Boyce were the only two Black reporters and were instrumental in helping the *Tribune* cover African American communities, including protest riots that erupted in the city following the April 4, 1968, assassination of the Rev. Dr. Martin Luther King, Jr.

When she left the *Tribune*, Johnson returned to Madison to get married. She also began working on a graduate degree, thinking she would teach journalism.

Later, Johnson's curiosity about how Black and white high school students communicated in the aftermath of the 1977 groundbreaking television miniseries *Roots*, based on Alex Haley's book, powered her doctoral dissertation. While researching her topic, a magazine editor asked her to attend a dinner with Haley. The meeting further framed her dissertation, "The Interpersonal Communications Effect of Viewing *Roots*: How High School Students Discuss Race Relations."

Born in 1945 in McAlester, Oklahoma, Johnson was an infant when her parents moved from the small town where her father was employed at the U.S. Naval Ammunition Depot. The family settled in suburban Evanston, Illinois, near Chicago, and Johnson, the oldest of five children, assumed responsibility at a young age. Her fifth-grade teacher took special notice of Johnson and asked her to babysit her toddler son. Before long, the teacher, Vera Brownlee, and her journalist husband, Les, became Johnson's second—and far more affluent—parents, taking her on vacations; exposing her to a wider circle of travel, culture, and people; and, ultimately, influencing her career path. Les Brownlee was a pioneering Black journalist in Chicago who worked for newspapers and television.

"My parents did what they could," Johnson said, proudly describing her housekeeper mother, Esther, and father, Elmer, whose postmilitary employment included bus driver, and house-painting and exterminating businesses. "If they had not raised me to be a responsible person, I would never have been asked to babysit and been exposed to a new world. Different people give you different experiences."

Reflecting on the several trails that she has blazed—from academia to publishing—Johnson knows that she has been fortunate. It wasn't merely that Johnson was in the right place at the right time. More often, she was the right person with the right timing for her assignments. Johnson recognizes that her professional ascent was no rung-by-rung climb up the career ladder. She may have skipped a few rungs, but her destination was still at an apex. She was a publisher.

"I've always come in at the top," Johnson said. "It's not great because you don't have anyone holding you up. So, if I had to ask a question about how to do something, I knew the response would be, 'She's the publisher, why doesn't she know that?'

"But you throw me in to sink or swim, and I'm going to swim. Think I can't do it? Watch this."

Finding herself on the business end of a communications company, Johnson's strategic processes expanded into maintaining quality journalism, while also making it profitable. She met with disgruntled advertisers and disgruntled staff, alike. She didn't put off offensive callers. She joined boards and community organizations, knowing membership and leadership built favorable relationships.

"There were three things that I wanted people at the paper to perceive in me. I knew that I had to be smart," said Johnson, long a reader of management how-to-books. "I wanted to be firm but fair. And I wanted them to see that I had power to get things done; the power to get them promoted. I put those goals on cards and put them on a mirror at home.

"After a while, the people who worked there were repeating what I had put on the cards about me."

She let the editors handle the newsroom but made her presence known and felt. One day, as she was strolling through the newsroom, Johnson noticed a reporter typing an interview quote that included "Jesus Christ" and his twelve "f—ing clowns."

The newsroom held its collective breath as Johnson leaned in and down. She simply said, to the reporter, "Do you think you can get the point across that he was irreverent with different language?" The reporter did.

Johnson's double majors in journalism and education reflect a double consciousness that has remained throughout her career. After serving as director of Western Kentucky School of Journalism and Broadcasting for seven years, she asked to be reassigned as a full-time professor in the school. While teaching full-time, she conducted research on how internships affect a journalist's career, and is also gathering research on African American women in management positions.

"I'm doing research [on the thesis] that successful Black women make the best managers because by force or choice, we've worked with all kinds of people," Johnson said, several months before she retired from the university in December 2020 and was inducted into the National Association of Black Journalists' 2020 Hall of Fame.

Continuing to reach out and help other students, journalists, mentors, and managers is important because Johnson has benefited in all these roles and in all these categories.

"Whoever's in my path, I help them because so many people helped me," Johnson said, "and they helped me with so many things that I could not have done." While Johnson's career contains enough chapters for several books, her zest for living and learning can best be marked by this footnote: "I'm 76, and I should have retired at 60, but these ideas still get me so excited."

Cathy Gant Hill is a freelance editor, writer and educator who worked twenty-two years as a reporter, including fourteen years covering arts, county government and consumer affairs for the Greensboro (NC) News and Record. *She lives in Greensboro, North Carolina.*

Chapter 19

Deborah Heard

Quiet Power in the Newsroom—Self-Possessed Manner
Guided Her Path to Management

It is nearly 5 p.m. on a Friday afternoon in Arlington, Virginia, about ten miles from the nation's capital. Because it is rush hour, anyone heading anywhere will, with certainty, be late.

Not Deborah Heard.

Seated in an oversized booth in the middle of the Carlyle, a popular restaurant that attracts a diverse mix of people who either live in the area or are just passing through, Heard is on time and unbothered by the busyness around her. Seeing Heard's easy, relaxed smile, it's hard to believe that a few years earlier, constant deadlines dictated her days as assistant managing editor at the *Washington Post*.

Truth Tellers: *The Power and Presence of Black Women Journalists Since 1960*

It had been too many years to count since I had last seen my dear friend, whom I met when we were Dow Jones Newspaper Fund interns in 1979. As wide-eyed graduates from our respective universities in North Carolina and Alabama, we were roommates that summer in Lehigh, Pennsylvania. Once our three-week training session ended, we would head to internships in other states far different from the South that raised us. Graduate school in even more distant places from home would follow our internships.

Heard's original plans, growing up in Heflin, Alabama, were to be an English teacher or a librarian. Suddenly, it all made sense that the quiet, soft-spoken young woman I met in 1979 would end up in the highest halls of power, massaging into shape all sorts of language, reporting, and rhetoric to be consumed by legions of *Washington Post* readers.

Heard's detour from high school literature and libraries came shortly before she transferred from Jacksonville State University to enroll in the University of Alabama.

Like many promising journalism students, Heard's writing abilities were noticed by one of her English professors. The professor contacted the editor of the local, the *Anniston Star* newspaper, and Heard got her first taste of what it was like to work for a newspaper.

"My path was different," she said. "I didn't want to be a reporter, and I didn't discover copyediting until the University of Alabama. I felt like being a copy editor was even better because I was paid to sit behind a terminal and read. This was 1979. I was still an introvert and learned to be an extrovert."

After earning her undergraduate degree in journalism, Heard's next stop was a copyediting summer internship with the Dow Jones Newspaper Fund. She later attended the University of Missouri for graduate school and worked as a summer intern for the *St. Paul Pioneer Press* before heading to the *Miami Herald*'s copy desk for a three-year

Deborah Heard at The Washington Post in 2005.

stint. In Miami, Heard served as editor of *Neighbors NW*, a twice-weekly community tabloid. She also was a copy editor and page editor.

Working in Miami was similar to her copy editing internship at the Pioneer Press; the *Herald's* copy desk was self-contained with just five to ten people, a natural "us [copy desk] against them [reporters, editors]" mentality was in play. She generally worked a 4 p.m. to 2 a.m. shift.

A different state of mind prevailed once Heard left Miami for Washington, D.C.

"The biggest thing for me was the shift from Miami to the *Washington Post*," said Heard. "In Miami, everything was loose and carefree. At the *Post*, things were not as carefree. In Miami, photographers wore shorts and flip-flops. I missed that about Miami, along with the teamwork. In D.C., everyone seemed to wear gray suits. The *Post* was so serious."

"In my first year at the *Post* [1984], I worked on the Metro Desk," she said.

"I was an assignment editor there for couple of years, then moved over to the Style section. In Style, I held a series of jobs: assignment editor, lifestyles editor, deputy assistant managing editor."

From 2005 to 2009, she was assistant managing editor of the *Post*'s award-winning Style section. That position meant deciding what events and people deserved coverage "in order to create a section that informed and entertained a diverse audience." Heard also was responsible for hiring and managing a staff that ranged from fifty to seventy-five employees, leading professional development seminars, and contributing to all aspects of newsroom-wide decision making.

While balancing such myriad roles, Heard remained keenly aware of being a young Black woman in a predominantly white newsroom at the center of the nation's—and the world's—power. "I was always very careful about how to walk through the newsroom—I walked through there like I was busy."

Yet, Heard believes her ability to handle the pressure was knowing that she was not alone.

"I was not an anomaly. The [*Miami*] *Herald* did a good job of promoting women. I never felt I was a groundbreaker. The only time was when I became the assistant managing editor for *Style*. She'd previously served as deputy assistant managing editor under David Von Drehle and Eugene Robinson, now a Washington Post associate editor and columnist who frequently appears on the *MSNBC* cable network. She described Robinson as "an incredible guy and an incredible editor."

After Robinson became a columnist, Heard landed the associate managing editor job, which was a first for a Black woman in *Style*. "*Style* was at its height: there were about seventy-five people working in the section," said Heard. "The most fulfilling part was seeing writers deliver stunning stories. My part in that was so tiny. That was really satisfying to be a part of this amazing work."

Heard also relished being able to help people find their own footing, do well, and thrive. She enjoyed creating a diverse pool of reporters, fighting for people to get raises, and helping young writers get the opportunities and attention they deserved.

"One of my staffers brought in his daughter to meet me because he wanted her to meet a female boss," she recalled, smiling.

Finding a mentor became a popular idea for women moving into or up the corporate ranks during the 1980s and 1990s and probably remains so today. Yet Heard said there was no one person that filled that role for her.

"There were people I trusted and relied on for different things," such as Milton Coleman and Shirley Carswell. Both worked in administrative and management positions. Coleman was a senior editor at the *Post* when he retired in 2012, and in 2020, Carswell became executive director of the Dow Jones News Fund, the organization that enabled me to meet Heard through our newsroom training in 1979.

Deborah Heard stands outside The Newseum before its Washington, D.C. location closed in 2019.

We briefly discussed those days that provided journalistic learning and training, and chuckled over incidents that were fun and sometimes frightening. After leaving the *Post*, Heard became executive director of the Zora Neale Hurston–Richard Wright Foundation, a literary nonprofit organization that discovers, mentors, and honors Black writers through workshops, master classes, public readings, competitions, and awards. Author Marita Golden and bibliophile Clyde McElvene created the foundation in 1990. No longer executive director of the foundation, Heard continues to serve on its board.

Four decades after penning her first news story, Heard's advice to women entering journalism echoes much of what she was told during the Dow Jones Editing Program under the late Sam Adams and others who helped coach her and the program's student journalists.

"Beyond the standard 'work hard,' you must have integrity, especially if you want to be a leader," she says. "Study and understand the culture. Don't get sucked into the gossip or part of the machine. Keep your mouth shut and listen until you figure it out."

She encourages young minorities to consider journalism management because it is important work. "It is the people in leadership who get to shape behaviors," she said.

"There were times that I kept things out of the paper. I think it is essential that we be there and the rewards have to be there. Yes, I loved it. It was so exciting. That is one reason I would encourage everybody to spend time on the copy desk. I learned how to judge photographs, what makes a good display, how packages come together. All of that experience helped me become a leader."

Chapter 20

Sandra Daye Hughes

Daring to Be Seen, Heard, and Respected—Building a Lasting, Illustrious Career at Her Hometown News Station

By Cathy Gant Hill

Sandra Daye Hughes spent her entire news career at one news station, in one location, and in one city. But because she started journalism so near the mountaintop, there was little left for her to prove by moving to other locales.

Much like the city of her provenance, Greensboro, North Carolina, and her alma mater, North Carolina A&T State University, Hughes also made history when she walked into the WFMY television station in 1972 and asked for a job. She was not the first African American to be on air at the local CBS affiliate—two others preceded her. Hughes, though, was the first African American woman to host a daily talk show at WFMY.

And the way that Hughes got her start is the stuff of legend. Hughes went to the station on an impulse. Well educated. Well spoken. Well dressed.

She got the job and nearly forty years later—in 2010—retired from it. Along the way, she has plowed through a series of achievements:

- In addition to hosting her own talk show, *Sandra and Friends*, she was also the first African American woman in the Southeast to host the nationally syndicated *PM Magazine* in 1978.

- She was the first female broadcaster asked to participate in the European Communities' Visitors Program, an invitation of travel and cultural immersion that Hughes considers a career highlight.

- The Greensboro Chamber of Commerce honored her with its Edward R. Murrow Award for news reporting in 1981, making her the first African American in the region to receive the award.

- The National Association of Black Journalists honored her with the Chuck Stone Lifetime Achievement Award, in memoriam to the pioneering newspaperman, in 2014.

- The International Civil Rights Center and Museum in 2006, the organization that memorializes the famous sit-in movement launched in Greensboro, North Carolina, selected Hughes as an Unsung Hero.

- Other notable awards include the Order of the Long Leaf Pine from the North Carolina Governor's Office, multiple "Best of Gannett" wins for news anchoring and programming, and a distinguished alumni award from NC A&T, which also later awarded her an honorary doctorate of humanities.

Hughes's climb to such heights did not come without hard work, heartache and sacrifice.

"We came from extremely low-lifestyles, no heat, no lights, no water, no [indoor] bathroom. No nothing in the house," Hughes recounted of her childhood. "But when I was almost 6, my dad wanted to go to A&T."

The family gave up tobacco farming and moved fifty miles west to Greensboro's Morningside public housing community. Her stepfather—Charlie Alfred Daye--found other work and eventually enrolled at North Carolina A&T to pursue his dream of a formal education. Just as determined was Hughes's mother who set behavioral standards that mandated: "When you go out of this house," Hughes recalls, "you act like folks."

Hughes's mother had her children baptized as Catholic so that they would have entrée into integrated parochial schools: Our Lady of Miraculous Medal, now St. Mary's, and Notre Dame High School. Next was college at what is now North Carolina A&T State University. Hughes graduated in 1969 with a bachelor's degree in English education and planned to teach high school students.

Discovering that most high school vacancies were for math teachers and unable to find work teaching, Hughes found an editing job at the Western Electric company. She stayed there two years, and by now married and pregnant with her first child, Hughes took time off. When she tried again for a teaching job, she had no better success than with her first search. Disappointed but not despairing, she drove down one of northeast Greensboro's main avenues lost in thought, and the TV station loomed ahead.

Hughes turned her car into the parking lot and went in. There she met her destiny.

It was 1972:

- Seven years since the 1965 Voting Rights Act was approved guaranteeing African Americans the right to vote;

- Twelve years since 1960, when four determined freshmen at her alma mater, North Carolina A&T, ignited a national sit-in movement for integrated public accommodations.

- Four years since the National Advisory Commission on Civil Disorders (the Kerner Commission) had decried the lack of racial diversity in newsrooms as an underlying factor in riots and other disturbances in twenty-five urban cities. Newspapers and television stations had ignored Black communities and issues or focused on only crime in minority communities, and when rioting in those communities took place in the 1960s, news organizations were ill equipped to cover the stories.

When Hughes walked in the door at WFMY that day, all that history came in too, on both sides of the reception desk.

"I'd like to apply for a job."

"A job? What kind of job?" came the derision-dripped reply.

"What kinds of jobs do you have?" was Hughes's cucumber-cool response, oiled with her mother's reminder to "act like folk."

As she filled out a one-page general application, with no specifics, the buzz about her presence must have rippled back to the newsroom and studio. The news director, perhaps still mindful of the Kerner Commission's findings, came out and asked Hughes if she had ever thought about being a reporter.

"He said, 'Think about it and I can teach you what to do,'" Hughes recalled. "And that was the beginning of my news career."

Nonetheless, it was not the Cinderella story of fables. Even though she was the third African American reporter to work at WFMY and even though it was the post–civil rights era of 1972, Hughes's early tenure was rocky. Calls, letters, complaints, and threats came daily, often laced with the N-word. White people tried to intimidate her when she was out covering stories; someone even roughly bumped her. Even some of the white male reporters could barely abide the notion of her next to them as an equal.

"The community hated the sight of me being on TV," Hughes recalled.

Still, she was thrilled in 1976 when she got her own talk show, *Sandra and Friends*. Much of the viewing community was not. Many

Black viewers objected that *Sandra and Friends* was not an all-Black forum. Bomb threats requiring the station to evacuate were called in so regularly—presumably by white viewers—that Hughes refused to leave the studio when most everyone else did.

"I had already been threatened so many times that the bomb threats were not much of a surprise," Hughes said. "I was stubborn enough that I wouldn't let them stop me. I would sit there and talk until the police came and gave us the sign.

"Since I had tried so hard to get a teaching job and that didn't work out, I believed that God intended for me to be at that TV station, that God intended me to do that as a way of helping people in my race move ahead a little."

She considered leaving the job, though, when callers would say that her daughter, Tiffany, had been hurt or was in trouble. Her co-workers had thawed and when the calls came when she was on air, one of them would rush to day care to ensure Tiffany's safety and report to Hughes. The most assurance came from the newswoman's family. Her late husband, Larry, her parents, in-laws, and a small circle of friends established a safety net, ensuring that any call regarding Tiffany's safety would come from one of them. *Go on and continue your career.*

Said Hughes: "I got beat up. I fought. I learned."

The animus had dwindled by the end of the decade. But when her three-year-old son, Larry Jr., drowned in the family swimming pool in the early 1980s and Hughes finally recovered well enough to return to reporting, she got nasty reminders of the early years. She got letters saying that her son's death was retribution for her daring to be seen, heard, and respected on television news. It seemed unbearable, but in addition to her family and friends, her co-workers now championed her, literally forming buffers around her if she were out on assignment.

It wasn't easy for Hughes's surviving children, Tiffany and Allan, who were picked on in school simply because their mother was a television news reporter and later an anchor. Yet, she and her husband taught them to withstand, *to act like folk*. Family is the reason that when other jobs came calling, Hughes didn't feel the challenge to prove her journalistic mettle in a bigger market.

"I thought, if I ever moved I would have to pay somebody to watch my children," says Hughes, crediting her mother, mother-in-law, and sister-in-law as steadfast caregivers for her children.

"It was important to me that they be looked after by people who loved them instead of people hired to watch over them."

Hughes, despite the trials, has been content to stay in the city whose history she has covered and has also been written into its pages. She has taught television production and journalism to students at A&T after retirement and then was called back to WFMY to anchor during the station's transition between permanent anchors. Now, she's a busy civic leader with grandchildren to tend. But going to the grocery store, the supermarket, or nearly any outing in Greensboro is to be back in the fishbowl for this reluctant big fish.

Shoving has been replaced with selfies by admiring viewers who remember the woman whose face and name were trusted to bring them information for forty years.

Cathy Gant Hill is a freelance editor, writer and educator who worked 14 years as a reporter covering arts, county government and consumer affairs for the Greensboro (NC) News & Record. She lives in Greensboro, North Carolina.

Chapter 21

Lynn Norment

Ebony Exclusives: From Al Green to Tina Turner—Determination, Grit Gave Her Rarefied Access to Black Celebrities

Like the colorful details that she revealed monthly about rich, famous and ordinary people, Lynn Norment's thirty-three-year-career as a writer and editor at *Ebony* magazine unfolded after she met John H. Johnson, the iconic magazine's founder and publisher, while in Chicago to attend a wedding in the mid-1970s.

Norment, who grew up reading *Ebony* and other publications that chronicled people who fascinated her, told Johnson that she would love to write for his magazine. At the time, she was a reporter for Memphis, Tennessee's daily newspaper, the *Commercial Appeal*.

Truth Tellers: *The Power and Presence of Black Women Journalists Since 1960*

She was hired as an *Ebony* freelancer and one of her first assignments was to write about Al Green, the legendary soul singer-turned minister. *Ebony* wanted a follow-up story on Green, who had been involved in a domestic violence incident two years earlier in October 1974. Green suffered third-degree burns when an admirer, Mary Woodson, threw a pot of boiling grits on him. The incident occurred at Green's home in Memphis, and Woodson reportedly committed suicide minutes after scalding Green. During his recovery from the burns, Green decided to abandon his secular singing career and focus on the ministry and gospel music.

"For the interview I met Al in East Memphis, and he drove me in his Rolls Royce to his farm in Oakland, Tennessee," Norment recalled. Green would not allow her to take notes during the interview. "I just tried to remember everything he said," she said. "When he took a break, I'd go into the bathroom and write down what he had said. I was reluctant to bring up the grits incident, thinking he might end the interview altogether. So, on the way back to Memphis I asked how the incident had affected his life. He told me he'd been born again and had founded a church. That information had not been published."

Although she was not looking for a job, the breaking news story was her winning ticket to Chicago and a full-time job at *Ebony* magazine. She also wrote a story about the interview for *The Commercial Appeal*.

Growing up in Bolivar, Tennessee, population 7,000, Norment saw her strong interest in reading and writing as "an escape" from the daily life of her hometown. Her mother died when she was 10, and her two older sisters ran the large household that totaled five daughters and their father. Her father remarried two years later and had another daughter. Norment also has three brothers.

Norment's father wanted at least one of his daughters to become a physician, but she decided that journalism was her calling. *Ebony* helped nurture her thirst.

"While growing up, *Ebony* opened my eyes to a larger world," she said. "It showed me that Black people were beautiful, accomplished and doing some incredible things. It gave me something to dream about and aspire to be."

Along with *Ebony* and other magazines, she *also* read Memphis's daily newspapers. She wrote for her high school and college newspapers, an experience that provided platforms for her career goals. Although Memphis State University's college journalism department was small, its instructors nurtured her journalism skills. Norment also had a good mentor who encouraged her to apply for an internship at *The Commercial Appeal*. She applied but was not hired. Her mentor insisted that she send her application again with her photograph.

"I did, and I got the job," said Norment.

Her first day as a professional journalist started out rather boring. She covered a speech and wrote three paragraphs. However, her boredom did not last long.

"As I prepared to go home around 6 p.m., all hell broke loose in the newsroom," she recalled. "A madman was shooting people in the street in a South Memphis neighborhood. The night editor yelled out my name and sent me out there by myself. He told me to find out as much information as I could about the shooter and the victims."

Norment got in her car and pulled out a map, for she had never been on that side of town, to that neighborhood. "I really was kind of afraid, for by then it was dark," she recalled. Then, while walking the streets and knocking on doors, her path crossed with that of a man whose family owned a funeral home in the area." The stranger helped her get her story by asking community residents to talk to her.

"He seemed to know everyone, and he told them to be nice to me."

The man turned out to be the future Congressman Harold E. Ford Sr. The next day, her byline made the front page with others who worked on the big story, and her father finally understood why she chose to become a journalist instead of a doctor.

Norment's flirtation with headline news was brief. Back on the obituary desk, she learned to be creative to avoid always writing about the dearly departed. With a white reporter, she proposed investigative projects, including an exposé on racism in rental apartment housing. When her articles ran, some in the white community were enraged.

"I received calls at home from people trying to get me to back down. One caller told my roommate, 'Your friend should not be publishing those stories.' I felt threatened but not afraid."

Norment continued to write about race and other topics for three years, and she won awards with her colleagues. Then *Ebony* hired her and she moved to Chicago, an eight-hour drive north of Memphis. At *Ebony*, Norment covered practically everything.

"I soon realized that to move ahead and get good assignments, I had to come up with great story ideas," she said. "People in the business community and entertainment industry began to trust me and pitch their ideas directly to me. They also would tell me everything, some off the record. They would get real."

But after arriving at *Ebony*, where she covered everything from business, religion, politics and lifestyles, Norment was faced with another reality: men ran the publication. She didn't find it odd because she didn't know many, if any, women in executive positions at any newspaper or magazine, she said.

Lynn Norment and the late Chicago Mayor Harold Washington.

"It took a while for me to find my spot," she explained during a meal in Chicago in 2015. "There were some who were jealous, who were naysayers, because I was getting exclusives.... I did stories on Reverend Benjamin Hooks, a Memphis native who headed the NAACP. I covered Harold Washington, the first Black mayor of Chicago."

Whitney Houston, the late legendary singer and actress, only wanted to talk to Norment. Prince requested that she interview him. Janet Jackson wanted to talk to her and her only. Spike Lee called her often in hopes of getting coverage on his films.

Norment felt that work brought a different perspective in a world ruled by men.

Despite her steady stream of attention-grabbing articles, some of Norment's male supervisors continued to downplay her role as a solid journalist.

"Mr. Johnson, the publisher, had to tell them to back off," Norment said. "The executive editor, managing editors … I had to fight those sexist battles, and sometimes they were intense. I would suggest stories on certain issues, and they would ignore me. Some of them tried harassing me simply out of jealousy. They would sit together and have coffee. It was clear that some felt threatened. Within the company, but not at *Ebony*, there were several women in executive positions who supported me."

Around the same time, Norment became active with the National Association of Black Journalists.

"I received a lot of support from the local chapter and NABJ national, from people like Paula Madison and Betty Baye." Madison, who started her career as a print reporter, went on to become a leading television news executive and strong proponent of newsroom diversity. Baye was a revered columnist for the *Louisville Courier Journal*.

"When Mr. Johnson wanted to promote me to a management position, others argued that I had no management experience. I later learned that Mr. Johnson told them, 'She's doing a great job managing the NABJ chapter and she'll do a great job managing here.'"

Among all the celebrities that Norment interviewed or covered, she considers the singer Tina Turner among the most notable "because of her strength."

"Growing up, I knew about Tina and Ike and I could relate," she said of Tina Turner's troubled marriage to Ike Turner, who created the popular 1970s band, the Ike and Tina Turner Revue. Tina grew up on a farm in a small Tennessee town not far from the small town in which Norment grew up. "When Tina and I met, we talked about our small towns. She said she always felt out of place, that she had to get out of there.

"I first interviewed Tina while she was in California before she moved to Europe. Years later I interviewed her in Germany and Denmark. That was memorable. She was always open and honest. I recall her telling me that she never used tap water on her face and that she was grateful for her legs. She also said that while growing up in Tennessee, her legs were considered skinny and not appealing."

Norment remains partial to her interviews with Al Green and Whitney Houston; she even attended and wrote an exclusive story on Houston's and Bobby Brown's wedding. She says that early on she had a great relationship with Houston, whom she met and interviewed at the beginning of her skyrocketing career. She also says she never felt comfortable writing about the escalating drug problems of the award-winning singer who died from a drug overdose in 2012.

"I knew she was having problems, but I kept thinking and hoping she would overcome them," said Norment. "That didn't happen."

Former President Barack Obama and former First Lady Michelle Obama, along with Beyoncé Knowles, Queen Latifah, Denzel Washington, Jennifer Hudson, Alicia Keys, Steve Harvey, Will Smith, Janet Jackson and dozens of other celebrities and famous figures were interviewed by Norment. In addition, she authored numerous columns for *Ebony*, including the Sounding Off music column and SisterSpeak opinion column, as well as producing countless *Ebony* photography sessions, including cover shoots.

When tapped as *Ebony*'s managing editor, Norment helped the publication establish a fresh voice and embrace new media. She left *Ebony* in 2009, four years after its creator, John Johnson, died.

"I had the greatest respect for him," Norment said of Johnson. "He was from Arkansas, I was from Tennessee. We could relate to our Southern roots. I recall a time when Mr. Johnson told me how much he liked Southern people on the staff because they were honest, good writers

Lynn Norment with members of the Association of Women Journalists in 2009.

and hard workers. And that if I knew of any other Southern journalists, to please refer them to him."

Looking back on the magazine that once was a staple in Black households everywhere but was sold twice and ceased publication of print copies, Norment says that she believes *Ebony* simply lost its key audience and failed to get a handle on the internet and digital media.

"You have to stay on top of the industry and be versatile and learn to adjust to the trends," she said.

Norment added another possible reason for *Ebony's* demise. When she arrived at *Ebony*, the magazine's focus was broader, with an emphasis on people from all walks of life, people from small towns such as Bolivar, her hometown, as well as factory workers and teachers, business leaders and academics.

Over the years, that focus shifted.

"I also feel that circulation started dropping because the magazine began specifically to focus on courting upwardly mobile and affluent young people." Such readers signaled a departure from *Ebony's* beginnings, said Norment.

"Mr. Johnson always knew and understood *Ebony's* audience, and he knew how to tell the *Ebony* story to potential advertisers."

Norment's work at *Ebony* was coupled with her work for NABJ and other journalism organizations. She was president of Memphis's Black media organization before she moved to Chicago, and was president of the Chicago NABJ chapter for six years. In 2009, Norment was inducted into the National Association of Black Journalists Hall of Fame in "recognition of her accomplishments and contributions to journalism." A former NABJ board member, she has chaired two conventions and continues to chair NABJ projects.

Norment's life and career have been documented in The *HistoryMakers* archives now housed in the U.S. Library of Congress, and she has been honored with the University of Memphis's Distinguished Alumna Award and the University of Memphis Journalism Department's Outstanding Journalism Alumna Award.

A special honor is her receipt of the 2020 John H. Johnson Day Award. Established by Friends of John H. Johnson as part of John H. Johnson Day in his home state Arkansas, the award "recognizes individuals who have made significant contributions in a way that embodies John H. Johnson."

Norment acknowledges that she had a "great career" at *Ebony*, which enabled her to travel to Africa, Europe and Brazil and throughout the United States. She advises young people aspiring to careers in the media to broaden their skills and consequently broaden their horizons.

"I always tell young people to make sure they are versatile and capable in all aspects of the media. No longer can you be just a writer or just a television reporter. You must be able to do it all. TV journalists must know how to write. Print journalists should know how to do a podcast or news broadcast. Everyone must be proficient in the digital aspects of the media, because if you want to succeed in the media, you must be able to do it all and be prepared for opportunities as they arise."

Chapter 22

Stacy Hawkins Adams

Charting a Path with Words That Resonate—Journalism Propelled Book Career and a Desire to Uplift Others

Much like fellow Arkansas native and renowned author and poet Maya Angelou, Stacy Hawkins Adams grew up wanting to tell great stories. And like Oprah, who grew up in neighboring Mississippi, Adams learned after years in the journalism business that she needed to expand her writing sphere and become a writing entrepreneur.

As a daughter of the South, author and journalist Adams was raised in a deeply spiritual community surrounded by teachers and family members who nurtured her storytelling abilities. In fact, her writing talent was discovered while she was in elementary school in her hometown of Pine Bluff.

Truth Tellers: *The Power and Presence of Black Women Journalists Since 1960*

"In fourth grade, my teacher asked me to write the class play for our school's annual talent show, and in fifth grade, my homeroom teacher mailed a poem that I penned about police officers to our local leaders, unbeknownst to me," Adams recalled, adding that the police chief wrote her a thank-you letter after hearing about the poem and offered her a tour of the police station.

"That was my first realization that my writing could have an impact," said Adams.

Her love for writing intensified, and by middle school, she was writing for a literary journal with the intention of one day becoming the next Angelou.

Adams's high school newspaper further aided her thirst for writing, and she occasionally scored opportunities to write freelance articles for her hometown's daily newspaper, the *Pine Bluff Commercial.*

With her love for writing still intact, after graduation Adams attended Jackson State University on an academic scholarship. During her four years as the historically Black institution in Jackson, Mississippi, she flourished as a budding journalist. She accepted a summer internship after her freshman year at the *Arkansas Gazette* in Little Rock, Arkansas. In her sophomore year, she was selected for a summer internship at *USA Today*, under the mentorship of Wanda Lloyd, one of the newspaper's African American senior editors (see chapter 8). Adams also was in the inaugural class of Chips Quinn Scholars, a minority student summer journalism program curated by the Freedom Forum that assigned her to the *Albuquerque Tribune* in New Mexico, and she served as the editor-in-chief of Jackson State's campus newspaper in both her junior and senior years.

In addition to developing an impressive assortment of clips, Adams gained many mentors along the way—in particular women of color at *USA Today*, including Barbara Reynolds, the only writer of color on the editorial board during the early 1990s; and Sharon Shahid, a researcher in the editorial department, who went on to be a lead writer for the Newseum and to serve as a freelance writer for exhibits now featured at the National Museum of African American History and Culture.

Women such as Reynolds, a former social worker-turned-journalist who also worked for the *Cleveland Press*, *Ebony* magazine, and the *Chicago Tribune*, entered the mainstream news business in the late 1960s, roughly around the time that the National Advisory Commission on Civil Disorders (also known as the Kerner Commission Report) was unveiled. The report blamed the nation's newsrooms for a lack of diversity among its ranks and illustrated how news was negatively skewed in coverage of poor Black communities.

Adams's ascension to the newsroom came more than two decades after Reynolds's and after the swell of Black men and women who became journalists in the mid- to late 1970s. Often they were the only Black journalists in their newsrooms, and many felt little connection to people, particularly Black professionals, who could provide them with career advice.

By the mid-1980s, mentorships were championed by the National Association of Black Journalists and other professional organizations. In such a competitive, anxiety-filled industry, experienced Black journalists helped new entrants navigate their careers. So, by the time that Adams entered the newsroom, things had improved, and she was lucky enough to have mentors who could help guide her journey.

Reynolds offered that support to Adams during the summer of 1991 when they worked together, and both Lloyd and Shahid remain friends and mentors with Adams today.

When Adams was interviewing for her first job in journalism during her senior year at Jackson State and homed in on several newspapers where Lloyd had professional connections, Lloyd willingly served as a reference and offered advice on salary negotiations.

Adams graduated from college a semester early in December 1992, and one month later began working full time as a night general assignment reporter at *Florida Today* in Melbourne, Florida, where her coverage included city council meetings. She stayed with the paper for ten months before being lured to Richmond by the opportunity to work in a larger market and cover an intriguing beat. She joined the staff of the *Richmond Times-Dispatch* as a suburban courts reporter, a position she held for three years. Adams was promoted to the social issues beat in 1996 and covered nonprofits and human service organizations, penned human interest stories, and reported on policy-related and breaking news stories.

In 2000, while still reporting, Adams was invited to add a weekly inspirational column to her duties to capitalize on the best-selling Chicken Soup for the Soul books franchise and the television hit *Touched by an Angel*. The column was a winner with readers, who, at one point ranked it as the number one reason they bought the Saturday edition of the *Times-Dispatch*, said Adams.

Her investigative reporting about a missing mother and child landed her on a segment of *The Montel Williams Show*, and another series of stories about Brittany Williams, a missing girl with AIDS, led to a nationwide search for Brittany and the federal imprisonment of the girl's caretaker.

Just as her journalism career at the *Times-Dispatch* evolved, so did a childhood dream. In 2004, while she was still working full time at the *Times-Dispatch*, married and raising two young children, Adams's first novel, *Speak to My Heart*, was published.

Like Oprah, she has continued to create her own path. After leaving full-time journalism in 2006, she went on to launch a freelance writing career with national clients, including *Heart & Soul* magazine, *AARP* magazine, and Crosswalk.com. The *Times-Dispatch* also hired her, securing her return as the newspaper's freelance parenting columnist (a position she held for ten years until early 2018).

When the national economy tanked in 2008 and magazines began to fold or shrink in size, Adams saw the need to make another shift. As an author assisting her publisher, she had gained an interest in the marketing aspect of writing and often assisted her publicist with promoting her books. With this interest in mind, she sought and obtained certification in nonprofit marketing and reached out to several of the nonprofits she had once covered on her newspaper beat to offer her marketing and writing services. She landed several clients, and as a marketing and

While reporting for The Richmond Times-Dispatch in Virginia, Stacy Hawkins Adams shared the print side of news for local television audiences from 1994-1996.

communications consultant, she went on to lead communications for a statewide nonprofit. Four years later, in 2012, she accepted a full-time marketing and communications offer to lead messaging for the largest private school in Richmond. Seven years into that role, she transitioned to a strategic marketing position in a quasi-governmental agency.

All the while, Adams has continued writing books and maintains a thriving author career in addition to her full-time strategic communications role. Today, she has eleven books under her belt: nine women's fiction novels, a nonfiction faith-based devotional book, and a book that is a compilation of original quotes. Other ventures include leading writing workshops, and developing a note card collection in collaboration with actress Daphne Maxwell Reid.

Mindful of the mentors who helped shape her career, Adams has faithfully paid it forward to future journalists. For several years she was a mentor for high school students who participated in the Richmond

Times-Dispatch-Dow Jones Urban Journalism Workshop, which ended several years ago after more than thirty years. She also helped mentor Times-Dispatch interns and younger writers who came through the newspaper or sought guidance from her through the Chips Quinn alumni program. And, as a Times-Dispatch columnist, she routinely visited secondary schools, colleges and universities to discuss her career path with students.

When aspiring journalists and others ask about her career path, Adams asserts that the unifying theme for all of her career moves has been her passion for writing and storytelling. In each evolution, those two factors have been the constant. And while she has not necessarily focused on writing about the Black community, she has brought stories about people of color and life as a woman of color to both mainstream and diverse audiences.

She also is grateful to live in a time where more journalists of color and female entrepreneurs of color have shown her a vision for taking her writing and storytelling to new levels of publication, brand building and product creation.

"The journalism of today is not what it was when I entered the field," said Adams. "Today, you have to go into it as an entrepreneur. You have to carve out a path that fits your passion and skills, while also meeting the needs of the culture and society for which you're writing and sharing stories. Even so, writing well is still vital, being accurate is still a must and storytelling is still a connecting force."

Chapter 23

Angela P. Dodson

A Window on Life and Death—Steely Reserve for Covering
Unspeakable Disasters in Places High and Low

On November 14, 1970, and for several weeks after, Huntington, West Virginia, was in shock. A chartered jet carrying most of Marshall University's football team, the coach, doctors, and athletic director, crashed while returning from a game against East Carolina University. Seventy-five people, including twenty-five boosters, many of whom were some of Huntington's most prominent citizens, were killed when the plane went down about two miles from the Tri-State Airport in Kenova, West Virginia.

Angela P. Dodson, who was a sophomore at Marshall when the crash occurred, had gone home to East Bank, West Virginia for the weekend, but decided to return to campus a day early. Her boyfriend picked her up, and when they stopped to get gasoline, the car's radio blared news about the crash. By the time she arrived on campus, "there was pandemonium" at the dorm.

"People were coming out of the dorm with mattresses for a makeshift clinic in the gym next door. I remember my dormitory floor mate telling me that her father, an assistant athletic director, was not on the plane. But I had five close Black friends who either were friends with or dated some of the football players. One friend was in pure agony. I can hear her screaming now."

As a journalism major, Dodson's class assignment was to cover the tragedy. While still in disbelief, she obliged, traveling to several of the players' funerals by bus with other Black students to Bluefield, West Virginia; Atlanta, Georgia; and South Carolina. Her articles appeared in the *Parthenon* student newspaper, and a documentary about the tragedy, *Ashes to Glory*, shows a photograph of Dodson attending a press conference.

"It was such a shock to all of us," said Dodson. "To lose that many people was just devastating. I interviewed some of the guys who missed the plane. There were a lot of individual stories that stood out and had to be told. It was just sad. A lot of students did not come back."

To cover one of the biggest stories of the year that would continue to make headlines decades later is rare for any journalist, much less a college sophomore. But for Dodson, who had known since she was 11 that she would one day be a journalist, her choice seemed prescient.

The Marshall story "reinforced my desire to be a journalist," she said. "It shaped a lot of my interests to the point that I love disaster coverage. Later in my career, when I was covering coal mine accidents, I'd be really focused on the details. "How did it blow up?' 'Where were the bodies?'"

After graduating from Marshall in 1973 and working for two years for the *Huntington Advertiser*, Dodson would go on to cover and edit stories for major newspapers that ultimately landed her as a senior editor of the *New York Times*, "the newspaper of record" and widely regarded for its influence and global readership.

Dodson's fondness for reading and writing was formed by the newspapers delivered to the homes where her family lived during her childhood. Born in Beckley, West Virginia, Dodson and her family moved to New Castle, Pennsylvania, when she was around age 2. Eight years later, her father's new job as an electronics technician for the Federal Aviation Commission required the family to move briefly to Oklahoma, before returning to Pennsylvania, this time to Meyersdale, a mostly white town in Somerset County.

Dodson was the only Black girl in her neighborhood, so she often found companionship by reading books, the *Pittsburgh Post Gazette*, the *Pittsburgh Courier*, and the Youngstown, Ohio newspaper. She also wrote poetry, a habit she started at age 7. By eighth grade, Dodson's father was transferred to Charleston, West Virginia, and the family settled in nearby Chesapeake. Her mother was determined to purchase a home in the area, resulting in news articles and local television cameras coming to their home, again whetting Dodson's appetite for the power of news.

Still, challenges arose. In junior high school, Dodson's teacher assigned her the task of writing about a fire that occurred near her home. After reading Dodson's paper, the teacher accused her of plagiarism, insisting that Dodson was using words that she could not possibly know. Dodson, who once read 120 books in a year while growing up, acknowledged that while she may have used one or two words that the newspaper used in describing the fire, everything else was her own.

The same teacher later placed another article written by Dodson into the school newspaper, and a few years later Dodson was named editor of her high school newspaper. Serving as editor of the newspaper, along with high school journalism classes, provided the guidance and structure that would prove pivotal for Dodson: her high school principal and one of her teachers both were former journalists.

"So, I had role models," she said. Her strong grades—"I was nearly always a straight-A student"— got the attention of school officials who encouraged her to apply to Marshall's journalism program, which had a strong reputation.

Rapid change was occurring in the journalism industry as a result of the 1968 Kerner Commission Report, which urged news organizations to more accurately cover Black people and the Black communities.

The *Charleston Gazette* and other newspapers were trying to recruit Black reporters, and by the end of her junior year in 1972, Dodson landed a summer internship as a copy editor. During her senior year, she learned that the *Huntington Advertiser* was trying to recruit a Black reporter; she was hired as a full-time reporter at the daily.

She covered education, features/art, and wrote about 100-year-old Callie J. Barnett, a well-known African American woman in Huntington, who was educator Carter G. Woodson's cousin. Dodson's article on Barnett, who lived to be 107, was prompted by Ernest Gaines's *The Autobiography of Miss Jane Pittman*, which was released in 1971 and later became a movie starring Cicely Tyson. In the book and movie, Jane Pittman, a former slave, becomes a civil rights activist who lived to be 107. Barnett's former home is listed in the *Green Book*, also known as "The Negro Motorist Green Book," an annual guidebook for African American road travelers, explained Dodson. Her articles about Black residents in Huntington garnered an Associated Press State Award, she added.

Unafraid to explore other stories, Dodson's coverage also included rural white school districts, Marshall's medical school, and interviews with celebrities with ties to Huntington such as the late comedian and television star Soupy Sales and Blaze Starr, a stripper and burlesque star, who was famous for having an affair with a former Louisiana governor Earl Long in the 1950s.

Dodson was a reporter at the Huntington paper from 1972 to 1974. After Huntington, she went to the Gannett Washington News Service

Angela P. Dodson

Angela P. Dodson (center) with Eugene Bribbroek, News Editor, and John C. Curly, Bureau Chief, Gannett News Services

as a correspondent on Capitol Hill where she covered agriculture, automobiles, mining, and regional issues in Ohio, Pennsylvania, Michigan, West Virginia, and New Jersey.

Dodson says all of this quickly and matter-of-factly with no hint of arrogance. Her conversations are peppered with dates, details, and add-ons that punctuate her fifty-year career. Two separate interviews with her stretched for nearly four hours and writing this piece took several days due to all the stories she shared and the time I spent reflecting on them.

NABJ was founded in 1975, just as Dodson was becoming acclimated in Washington. Yet, she didn't learn about the organization that advocated for the advancement of Black journalism professionals until 1977 when it hosted its annual meeting in Baltimore.

"The notion that this organization existed ... that was exciting. I met so many people there," she recalled. "It was very interesting. Up until that point, I may never have worked with anybody Black."

Although she is not an NABJ founder, Dodson describes herself as a 'near' founder. Several of NABJ's forty-five founders mainly signed papers, leaving the organizational work to "a whole group of us who got it off the ground and wrote the organization's constitution," she said.

The late *Philadelphia Inquirer* columnist and Pulitzer Prize winner Acel Moore had a big party during the Baltimore convention. Her husband, Michael Days, claimed that the two of them met at the party. Regardless where they met, the couple eventually became husband and wife.

Dodson remained at the Gannett Bureau as a part-time editor while attending graduate school at American University from 1978 to 1979. She worked as an intern, a requirement of her graduate program, at the *Rochester Times Union* in Rochester, New York, from 1979 to 1980. She returned to Washington in 1980 and worked for the *Washington Star*.

"I loved the *Star*," she said. "It was one of the most exciting places! I was the features editor for Washington Life and responsible for design, decisions for the late copy, much of it about late-night parties." Dodson occasionally attended some of the parties, and sometimes would leave a party and walk into the newspaper's composing room wearing a ball gown.

"When I first went there, I was the night editor on night side, but soon after I was promoted" to lead editor. I was there when John Lennon was shot. We had to cover parties like they were news. There were always breaking stories."

Dodson's tenure at the *Washington Star* didn't last long. The paper that was founded in 1852 and often was considered better than the *Washington Post* and other local papers, met its demise in 1981.

But the *Louisville Courier-Journal* had already recruited Dodson for its copyediting desk before the *Star* folded. The process of moving to Louisville involved two courtships: the *Journal* wooing Dodson partly because "it had gotten wind that I was dating Michael," she said, adding that her soon-to-be husband already was at the *Courier-Journal*.

Dodson's fast-track rise in the industry did not pause in Louisville. While working in Louisville between 1981 and 1983, she received a call from the *New York Times*. Even though she and Days had recently married and purchased a home, her husband persuaded her to take the job that most journalists consider to be the opportunity of a lifetime.

"I got to New York right after Thanksgiving in 1983 as a copy editor on the National Desk," said Dodson. "National elections were approaching." She soon was promoted to editor for the Living section and head of the Style Department. In 1992, Dodson became the first African American woman promoted to be a senior editor at the *New York Times*.

Around the same time, other African Americans such as Mary Curtis, C. Gerald Fraser, Paul Delaney, Rosemary Bray, Brett Pulley, Thomas Morgan, Dana Canedy, Lena Williams, and DeWayne Draften worked at the newspaper, forming what Dodson describes as a constellation of Black journalists.

Stars in a constellation change slowly over time and eventually are unrecognizable. At the *New York Times*, the end for Dodson came in the form of a lawsuit.

"At one point I decided that I needed to take a leave and get the hell out of there. A lot of my circle of support was shrinking. I was working with a lot of people who caused stress and tension, and I'd had a bad case of carpal tunnel. Being off a year gave me time to address it. Then I had surgery on both hands. Before it was time for me to go back, they were going to put me in a job on the news desk. They called it the "bull pen," and it would have caused a lot of stress. They said that I would not have to type, but it still was [situated] in the worst condition with the worst hours. Basically, I protested that they pressured me. I was being pressured to resign. I filed a lawsuit. Eventually we settled."

Dodson's lawsuit came nearly twenty years after a "huge" lawsuit African Americans filed against the *New York Times*. Many of the journalists involved in the suit left the newspaper, she said.

Yet, working for what is easily perceived as the world's leading newspaper did have its perks, Dodson acknowledged.

"It affords us a window on life. There is always something as a journalist that is intrinsically interesting. The people you meet. You meet famous people and learn from them and are inspired by them. I essentially have met every single president or been in their presence, starting with John F. Kennedy who came to New Castle when I was 10 and my parents took us to a rally.

"You also get to work for a premier news organization . . . to work with really good writers. You learn a lot, people look up to you, you're invited to speak, teach, attend workshops, and travel."

In 1991, Dodson and her husband, who by then was vice president for diversity and inclusion for the *Philadelphia Inquirer*, adopted four brothers who were then ages 4, 5, 6, and 9. Two of the children had special needs. Despite the demands and juggling required while working and running a household of four boys, the couple managed.

Angela Dodson during a 2017 author event in Richmond, Virginia. She is shown with relatives (from left) Dorothy Rice, Sonja Branch-Wilson and Muriel Miller Branch.

She advises women entering today's newsrooms to try to maintain balance in their lives. "Gerald Boyd [former managing editor of the *New York Times who died in 2006 at age 56*] used to say that the *Times* was his life," says Dodson. "You can never make a job your life. You can give it time, but you can't give it your life.

"The *Times* sucked up so much of my life. You got up, you go to work, and only have an hour for lunch. The commute was such a big part of it… ninety minutes to get out of Manhattan. There was no time to exercise or to belong to an organization, church, or sorority. At least I had a family, but once I had a family, it worked against me."

Since leaving the *Times*, Dodson balances life as a book editor and author. In 2017, her book *Remember the Ladies* was published. It documents milestones in women's hard-won struggle securing the right to vote and reflects on women's impact on politics since. Dodson also worked with fellow journalist Dorothy Gilliam on her book 2019 book *Trailblazer: A Pioneering Journalist's Fight to Make the Media Look More Like America*, along with husband's book *Obama's Legacy: What He Accomplished as President*.

"I look forward to more book projects and to travel with my husband who retired after forty-two years in journalism," she said.

Chapter 24

Yanick Rice Lamb

Considering All Things and More—Empathy for the Voiceless Guides Her Purpose

A passion for English and art thrives at the center of Yanick Rice Lamb's path as an author, journalist, magazine editor, and educator. Right from the start, Lamb saw writing as a way to speak out, recalling a time in high school where she was upset enough to write a letter to the editor. Her desire to use her voice to aid others continues to drive her.

Growing up in Akron, Ohio, among the rubber factories, Lamb credits her strong work ethic to parents who stressed education and good careers to their eldest daughter and her younger siblings. Her father,

William Rice, had a long career in the military and as a professor. After their divorce, her mother, Carmelie Jordan, often worked double shifts as a licensed practical nurse through the Visiting Nurse Service and later nursing homes, combined with private duty to care for individual patients. She also was a member of the Akron Black Nurses Association. For as long as she remembers, Lamb says she has tried "to be everything I could be," looking to heed her parents' message and turn her passions into a career.

As a student at Ohio State University from 1976 to 1980, Lamb found abundant opportunities related to her interests in communications. A sophomore year trip to Washington, D.C., to attend Howard University's Annual Communications Conference resulted in a chance meeting with Al Fitzpatrick, executive editor of the *Akron Beacon Journal*.

"I was at Knight Ridder's booth and a recruiter asked me if I knew Al," Lamb recalled. "I said that I hadn't met him yet, but that I went to school with his daughters. Then I heard a voice behind me ask, 'What are their names?' From that moment, he became my mentor and advised me about internships, jobs and the finer points of journalism."

Lamb was inspired to study journalism because she saw few people on television news who looked like her. Intentional about her plans to one day work as a journalist, she began writing for *Our Choking Times*, a Black campus monthly, the *Lantern*, the campus daily, and for community publications such as the *Onyx* and the *Call & Post*, as well as two local Black magazines. Lamb also became president of Ohio State's Black Communicators Association, which had a local member of the National Association of Black Journalists as its adviser. In June 1980, she graduated with a bachelor's degree in journalism.

"I think people who came [to journalism school at Ohio State] were mission-driven and upperclassmen had a big impact on us. I learned a lot from them," Lamb said. "Journalism was something I always thought was fascinating because it enabled you to learn something new every day."

A story that sticks with Lamb is one she wrote about a person with quadriplegia. She liked the idea of communicating about the experiences and issues of others. Lamb's empathy for the voiceless and desire to spread knowledge to help and empower others would ultimately lead her to journalism's highest realms of power, including the *New York Times* and appearances on numerous national and regional television and radio news outlets.

But before any of those hallowed halls were within reach, Lamb paid her dues by working in smaller newsrooms such as the *Toledo Blade* as a copy editor and reporter, before moving on to the *Atlanta Journal-Constitution*.

Lamb lists William Brower, associate editor and columnist at the *Toledo Blade*, as a mentor and someone who helped guide her early career. She started at the paper shortly after another Black, female reporter, Janet Cooke, had moved on to the *Washington Post*. Cooke would become infamous for an article she wrote "Jimmy's World." The story about an 8-year-old heroin addict was awarded the 1981 Pulitzer Prize in Feature Writing; however, it was later returned when Cooke admitted that the story had been fabricated.

"When the Pulitzer Prizes were announced, everybody was patting themselves on the back," Lamb recalls.

But when Cooke's story imploded, Lamb was worried what it might mean for her as a young, Black woman coming from the same paper.

"Janet Cooke was from the *Blade*. She was a good writer, just not a good journalist," Lamb continued. "I didn't encounter any problems, but I was aware later that Black journalists encountered more scrutiny overall around the country."

As she continued her career path, Lamb met many of the more established Black journalists—perhaps even the first wave of Black journalists who had entered the nation's mainstream newsrooms a decade or so before Lamb and her contemporaries. Names such as Jay Harris, Phillip Dixon, Michael Days, and Angela Dodson were well established in Rochester, New York, Washington D.C., and Philadelphia, along with mentor Pamela McAllister Johnson, the first Black woman to become publisher of a daily newspaper, the *Ithaca Journal*. The Howard communications conferences that she attended as a college student had also introduced her to Robert C. Maynard, the first African American editor and owner of a major daily newspaper in the United States—the *Oakland Tribune*, and Max Robinson, the first African American to anchor a nightly network newscast.

At age 26, Lamb landed at the *New York Times*. It was June 1984, and she describes her next ten years working there as exciting.

"A lot of African Americans were starting to come to the paper and the *New York Times* was at the top of its game," she says, ticking off the names of other African American reporters with whom she worked.

"Isabel Wilkerson, Lena Williams, William "Bill" Rhoden, Paul Delaney, Gerald Fraser, Angela Dodson, Rosemary Bray, E. R. Shipp, and Shawn Kennedy."

As laudable as all those names appear, Lamb quickly added that "Newsday had more."

But who's counting?

Actually, everyone. It was less than a decade before Lamb began working at the *Times* that the American Society of News Editors (ASNE) appointed its first Minorities Committee in 1977. The following year, the committee's first chair recommended an urgent focus on increasing the percentage of minority journalists and executives, with the goal of having the nation's newsrooms reflect the proportions of minorities in the total population before the year 2000.

"ASNE never met the goals of parity. It's a shame after a half-century," Lamb said. "At the end of the day, companies still aren't hiring and promoting enough people who look like us."

Despite whatever gains were being made or lost during this time, journalists such as Lamb never lost sight of their purpose. They came to work each day—leaving behind husbands, wives, parents, children, and often civic and social lives- to gather, to report the news for readers who were mostly unaware of the obstacles these Black journalists endured daily in their newsrooms.

"I think a lot of us made a difference holding managements' feet to the fire," Lamb said. "Plus, the community had our back. They knew where we needed to be and that we can't work in a vacuum. A woman once stopped me on the street and said, 'Thanks.' This was for my work as NYABJ president [New York Association of Black Journalists] and in journalism."

When Lamb's son, Brandon, was born, she switched from the news desk to regional news at the *Times* so she would be able to work during the day and be home with her son at night.

"Being a journalist and a parent is always a juggling act with all the deadlines and crazy schedules," Lamb said. "My family always came first though. I remember someone questioning certain events that I skipped. On one occasion, I said that no one would remember that I didn't attend a promotional event, but that my son would never forget if I missed an important game or school activity. I believed it was important to make my presence felt at his schools, to be a chaperone and to volunteer in the library."

While Lamb remembers the decade she spent at the *Times* as a "good experience overall," she acknowledged that "it had its ups and downs like any place." Sometimes there was tension behind the scenes in the newsroom, especially for Black and female journalists back then.

"Some felt like we were there because we knew what we were doing. Others felt like it was some sort of handout. Some felt 'we' had taken their spots," Lamb recalled. "Sometimes you had people who weren't used to working for an African American. On the whole, the corps of African Americans were extremely talented. You were not going to be mediocre."

Lamb said some of the highlights for African Americans working at the *Times* came when Isabel Wilkerson won the 1994 Pulitzer Prize in Feature Writing for a package of stories that included her profile of Nicholas, a fourth-grader from Chicago's South Side, and when Angela Dodson became the paper's Style editor. Personal triumphs came when readers or sources simply picked up the phone to compliment a staff member for his or her work.

"It was gratifying when people in the community would call you at the paper and say 'I saw your fingerprints'," Lamb said. "I tried to stay involved in the community. I always believed in the community. You have to sit down sometimes and talk about why you were upset with the story."

Lamb enjoyed her work for the newspaper and appreciated the resources the paper provided and working in a place that everyone else was following. But she eventually felt that she was hitting a glass ceiling. In 1992, she transferred to *Child Magazine* in the company's magazine division, where she was a senior editor, overseeing its coverage of family dynamics, education, politics, health and food.

After *Child* was acquired by Gruner & Jahr, Lamb left and soon became an editor-at-large for *Essence* magazine. On her first day, Lamb met with Robert Johnson and Debra Lee and discussed a BET project. She presented her ideas, then began developing the concept for BET Sunday, which evolved into *BET Weekend* magazine.

"One of my career highlights was serving as founding editor of *BET Weekend* magazine," Lamb said, noting that while building it from scratch was hard work, it was also a lot of fun. "It was my lifelong dream to start a magazine. [We had] a great team who worked hard and played hard... readers loved it, which was immensely gratifying."

Circulation grew from 800,000 to 1.3 million in three years, and when BET purchased *Heart & Soul* magazines in 1998, Lamb was promoted to editorial director and ran both publications. A few years later, the company began spinning off units and the magazine division became part of Vanguarde Media. While trying to choose between moving back to New York with Vanguarde, or staying in D.C., a new opportunity arose—teaching.

"Howard [University] was looking for someone with a newspaper and magazine background," Lamb said. "Teaching had been in the back of my mind since second grade, and now I started giving it serious thought—sooner than anticipated—but it turned out to be the right decision at the right time."

And while Lamb said that her experience as a founding editor with *BET Weekend* Magazine was fun, it is teaching at Howard University since 2001 that has proven most fulfilling.

"I'm approaching my twentieth anniversary," Lamb said in 2021. "I tell students how much they're needed everywhere, to be excellent, to be flexible and to know their worth. I tell them we're in a media revolution that's just as impactful as the birth of radio or television. I tell them that no one has really figured it out, which means that they can help to lead the way."

Reflecting on journalism's place in the digital media world that now exists, Lamb likes to quote Paula Matabane, her former Howard University colleague, in helping her students and her course curricula stay current.

"We do what we teach and teach what we do," the retired Matabane once told her.

"It basically means that I try to keep my skills and teaching fresh by doing journalism and teaching journalism," Lamb said.

In addition to her teaching schedule, Lamb continues to consult and freelance for several companies and organizations as president of Miyan Communications Group. She has written a series on environmental health that is being jointly published by the Center for Public Integrity and Belt Magazine, and is completing a doctorate in medical sociology to complement her ongoing work in health and science journalism. She is also a co-founder and publisher of the website FierceforBlackWomen.com.

"I don't think print is dead; I think it's different [and] you need good writers," Lamb said. "My point is that people still read—just in a different format. And they will read a story of any length if it's good."

Epilogue

America's current wave of civil, human, political, and social unrest echoes the protests and violence experienced by the country nearly fifty-five years ago. Just as the death of the Reverend Dr. Martin Luther King, Jr., sparked fiery protests, similar unrest occurred after the death of George Floyd, a Black Minnesotan who was choked to death by Derek Chauvin, a white police officer in Minneapolis on Memorial Day 2020.

Since that horrific event, reported by Black, brown, and white journalists everywhere, the U.S. government and numerous American corporations have vowed to do better. Confederate statues and symbols, along with other overt expressions of white supremacy, have been dismantled, including the Robert E. Lee statue in Richmond, the former capital of the Confederacy where I have lived since 1981. When a Black-owned Virginia construction company arrived to take down the Lee statue in September 2021, it was accompanied by the words of John Mitchell, Jr., the publisher and editor of Richmond's once leading Black newspaper, *The Richmond Planet*.

Mitchell wrote that the Lee statue, erected in 1890, would one day be taken down by a Black man. "He put up the Lee monument, and should the time come, will be there to take it down."

Poetic justice indeed.

In terms of promises for a more just and equitable society made by political and corporate leaders after George Floyd's murder, some advances have unfolded. Several mainstream news organizations renewed efforts to diversify their ranks and be more inclusive. In 2021, several African American men and women assumed key leadership roles at ABC News (Kimberly Godwin) and MSNBC (Rashida Jones). In 2020, Joy Reid moved into a primetime anchor seat on MSNBC to host *The Reid Out*, succeeding longtime host Chris Matthews, a white male who occupied the 7 p.m. chair for twenty-three years until his departure in 2020. A cadre of talented millennial Black women also emerged, including Errin Haines, a rising star in MSNBC's line of political commentaries, as well as an editor and founder of The 19th, a nonprofit news outlet. Tiffany D. Cross also earned her own seat at MSNBC with *The Cross Connection*, which aired on Saturday mornings before her contract abruptly ended before midterm elections in November 2022. And at CNN, that network's Abby Phillip is senior political correspondent and anchor of *Inside Politics Sunday*, an hour-long program featuring a panel of top-tier political analysts. Gayle King and Tamron Hall, both of whom cut their teeth in newsrooms, now lead CBS's venerable morning show and a syndicated midday talk show, respectively. Hall, who was shabbily treated by NBC, now has a leading daytime talk show. Not to be overlooked is Black women's continued emergence in national print operations, holding key editorial and decision-making roles at the *New York Times*, *Washington Post*, the *Miami Herald* (Monica Richardson), the *Houston Chronicle* (Maria Reeve), and the *Dallas Morning News* (Katrice Hardy).

In Richmond, Virginia, my former employer, the *Richmond Times-Dispatch*, hired Lisa Vernon Sparks, the first African American woman to serve on its Opinions Team as an opinion writer. Progress indeed. That "progress" did not last long as Vernon Sparks was among several newsroom staffers who were laid off in April 2022 when new leadership arrived at the newspaper. (Fortunately, Vernon Sparks, a talented reporter and writer immediately landed a new reporting job at the *Charlotte Observer*.)

Further, the *New York Times*'s prolific reporter Nikole Hannah-Jones, who covers racial injustice, was awarded a 2020 Pulitzer Prize for the *New York Times Magazine*'s landmark 1619 Project, which challenges U.S. history by marking the year when the first enslaved Africans arrived on Virginia soil as the nation's foundational date. A year after winning the Pulitzer, Hannah-Jones again garnered global headlines when she was courted by the University of North Carolina at Chapel Hill for a tenured teaching position, only to be rejected by the institution in which she earned a master's degree in journalism after a newspaper baron who donated millions to UNC's journalism school raised objections about granting her tenure.

Although Hannah-Jones eventually was offered tenure at the school, she turned it down in favor of Howard University. "It's pretty clear that my tenure was not taken up because of political opposition, because of discriminatory views against my viewpoint and, I believe, [because of] my race and my gender," Hannah-Jones said in published news reports.

Like so many other Black women journalists throughout the nation and the world, Hannah-Jones's commitment to journalism and truth telling is clear. In addition to her work for the *New York Times* and Howard University, in 2016 she co-founded the Ida B. Wells Society for Investigative Reporting, a training and mentorship organization dedicated to increasing the ranks of investigative reporters of color. Ironically, it is housed at UNC's Hussman School of Journalism and Media.

The greatest promise of all, perhaps, was delivered during the 2021 Pulitzer Prize awards when then Darnella Frazier won the citation "for courageously recording the murder of George Floyd, a video that spurred protests against police brutality." Frazier, then age 16, was not a journalist when she recorded her video, but her disbelief and outrage at seeing such a heinous act gave her the courage to document the vicious attack against a Black men accused of giving a convenience store clerk a counterfeit twenty-dollar bill. In recording Floyd's murder, Frazier did what Ida B. Wells-Barnett, Ethel Payne, and Alice Allison Dunnigan had done decades earlier in telling the stories of Americans who constantly were subjugated to second-class status and even murdered merely because of their Black and brown skins.

Dunnigan, the first African American female correspondent to receive White House credentials, also was the first Black female member of the U.S. Senate and House of Representatives press galleries. She covered Harry Truman's 1948 presidential campaign, another first for an African American female journalist.

Yet, later, under President Dwight Eisenhower's administration, Dunnigan often was overlooked in press briefings, an abusive and disrespectful practice that April Ryan, a veteran White House Press Corps member, experienced decades later under the Donald Trump presidency.

Dunnigan and Ryan were undaunted.

"Without Black writers, the world would perhaps never have known of the chicanery, shenanigans, and buffoonery employed by those in high places to keep the Black man in his proverbial place by relegating him to second-class citizenship," Dunnigan wrote in her 1974 autobiography, *Alone Atop of the Hill*.

With the election of President John F. Kennedy, Dunnigan became the first Black reporter to ask him a question during his first nationally televised press conference in 1961.

INDEX

Note: Photographs are identified by italicized page numbers.

AARP magazine, 178
ABC News, 142, 197
Accrediting Council on Education for Journalism and Mass Communications, 68, 141–142
Adams, Frank M., 19–20
Adams, Nettie Ruth Ivory, 19
Adams, Sam, 159
Adams, Stacy Hawkins, 175–180
   career of, 176–180
   education, training, and internships of, 175–176, *177*
   mentorships, 176–177, 179–180
   observations on writing career, 180
   personal history of, 175–176, 178
   photographs of, *175*, *179*
   racial issues and, 176–177, 180
Adams-Wade, Norma, 17–25
   awards and recognition for, 24
   Black community reporting by, 21–22, 25
   Black journalists influencing, 19, 21, 22–23
   career of, 19–25
   civil rights events influencing, xxi, 17–19, 21, 24
   education, training, and internships of, 17–18, 19–20, 21
   Maynard Institute and, 23–24
   NABJ and, 22–23, 24
   personal history of, 19–20, 23
   photographs of, *17*, *18*, *23*
   racial issues and, 20–22, 24–25
Adelstein, Gene, 79, 83
affirmative action, 40, 45, 106, 123, 134, 139–140, 147
Akili, Amber, 23–24
Akron Beacon Journal, 191
Al-Amin, Jamil Abdullah (formerly H. Rap Brown), 106
Albuquerque Tribune, 5, 176
Alfred I. DuPont–Columbia University Award, 137
Alliance for Colorado Theater Service to the Profession award, 91
Alone Atop of the Hill (Dunnigan), 200
American Nazi Party, 107
American Newspaper Publishers Association, 149
American Press Institute, 149
American Society of Newspaper [News] Editors, 66, 68, 130, 193
American Theater Critics Association, 92
American University, 186
Andrews, Julie, 90
And the Angels Sing column (Stone), 32
Angelou, Maya, 15, 90, 99, 141, 175, 176
Anniston Star, 156

Index

Ansa, Tina McElroy, 68
AP. *See* Associated Press
Aplin-Brownlee, Vivian, 73
"Are We There Yet?" (Varner, co-author), 40, 45
Arkansas Gazette, 176
Army and Air Force Exchange Service, 58
Ashes to Glory, 182
Associated Press (AP)
    awards and recognition by, 81, 120, 184
    Bridges at, 4
    racial discrimination complaints and lawsuit against, 134–135
    Ross at, 127–135
    Styles sourcing from, 137
Associated Press Managing Editors, 66
Atlanta Constitution, 129
Atlanta Daily World, 129
Atlanta Journal, 57, 61
Atlanta Journal-Constitution, 130, 192
Atlanta University Center, 132
Atlanta Voice, 129
Augusta Chronicle, 12
Augusta riots, 9–10, 11
Autobiography of Miss Jane Pittman, The (Gaines), 184

Baldwin, James, 103
Ball, Lucille, 139
Barnes, Claude, 105
Barnett, Callie J., 184
Barry, Marion, 40, 44
Baye, Betty, 171
Beach Beacon, 58–59

Belt Magazine, 196
Bennett College, 104, 141
Berkshire Hathaway, 35
Better Homes and Gardens, 100
Bettis, Ms., 122
BET Weekend magazine, 195
Birmingham bombing, xxi, 18
Bishop College, 25
Black Communicators Association, 191
Black Enterprise, 71, 149
Black Ink, 106
Black Lives Matter Plaza, 26–27, 30–31
Black Lives Matter protests, 27, 30–31
Black MBA Magazine, 33
Black Panthers, 72, 91
Black Press, xxii, 27
"Blacks in America" (Styles, contributor), 137–138, 143
Black Student Movement, 107
Black Teacher and the Dramatic Arts: A Dialogue, Bibliography, and Anthology, The, 89
Black Vibrations, 89
Black Women Unmuted, 135
Bloom Advertising, 21
Bond, Julian, 131
Boyce, Joe, 151
Boyd, Gerald, 188–189
Bradlee, Ben, 39–40, 63–64, 74
Bradley, Ed, *83*, 137–138
Bray, Rosemary, 187, 193
Bribboek, Eugene, *185*
Bridges, Denise, 1–8
    Black journalists influencing, xxii, 2, 3
    career of, 4–8

Index

education, training, and internships of, 2–4, 5
   Maynard Institute and, 4, 5, 7
   observations on journalism, 7–8
   personal history of, 1–2, 5, 6, 7
   photographs of, *1*, *5*
broadcast media. *See also specific news organizations*
   Ciara's work in, 78–85
   civil rights movement coverage by, xxiii–xxiv
   current diversity and inclusion in, 197–198
   Farmer's work in, 34
   Henderson's work in, 112–114
   Hughes's work in, 161–166
   Johnson's work in, 148
   Kennedy assassination coverage by, 18
   Kerner Commission Report influence on, xxv, 164
   layoffs and downsizing in, 79
   Styles's work in, 136–143
   Varner's work in, 43
   Walker's work in, 118–126
   Watts riots coverage by, xxii, 2
Brower, William, 192
Brown, Bobby, 172
Brown Angel Center, 76
Brownlee, Les, 152
Brownlee, Vera, 152
Buell Theater, 90
Bunn, Curtis, 76
Burlington Times-News, 14
Bush, George W., 80, 127–128
Butler, Adee Conklin, 28
Butler, Jessie Mae Norment, 28

Caldwell, Earl, 60, 72
California Teachers Association, 4
Call & Post, 191
Candy Wholesaler Magazine, 43
Canedy, Dana, 187
Carper, Elsie, 61
Carswell, Shirley, 159
Carter, Jimmy, 136
Cascade Public Media, 41, 47
CBS
   CBS News, 80, 140
   CBS News Sunday Morning, 140
   CBS Reports, 137, 140
   Charlie & Co. on, 111
   Ciara's work for, 80
   Cronkite at, 18
   current diversity and inclusion at, 198
   Hughes at, 161–166
   Johnson at, 151
   60 Minutes, 80, 137, 140
   Styles at, 136–138, 139–140
Center for Public Integrity, 196
Charles, Nick, 76
Charleston Gazette, 184
Charlie & Co., 111
Charlotte Museum of History, 15
Charlotte News, 71
Charlotte (NC) Observer
   Black women leaders at, 142
   Flono at, 10, 13–14, 15
   Israel at, 108–109
   Solomon at, 49, 52–54
   Vernon Sparks at, 198
Charlotte Women's History Hall of Fame, 15
Charlotte YWCA Women of Achievement Pioneer Award, 15

Index

Chauvin, Derek, 24, 125, 197
Chicago Media Group, 49
Chicago Sun Times, 102
Chicago Tribune, 49, 54–55, 151, 177
Child Magazine, 195
Chips Quinn Scholars, 176, 180
Chisman, Tom, 79
Chuck Stone Lifetime Achievement Award, 162
Church Hill (Richmond), 119–120, 121
Ciara, Barbara, 78–85
    awards and recognition for, 80–81
    career of, 78–85
    education and training of, 79, 82–84
    legacy of, 78, 85
    NABJ and, 81
    personal history of, 78–79, 81–83, 84–85
    photographs of, *78, 80, 83, 84*
    racial issues and, 79–81, 84
CIA's Secret Army, The, 143
Cincinnati Post, 114
Civil Rights Act of 1964, xxiii, 40
civil rights movement
    Adams-Wade influenced by, xxi, 17–19, 21, 24
    current protests echoing, 197
    Gilliam's coverage of, 28–29
    Hughes's opportunities influenced by, 162, 163–164
    Israel influenced by, 104–105
    March on Washington for Jobs and Freedom, xxi, 17, 40
    Montgomery Bus Boycott, xxiii, 67, 97–98
    news media coverage of, xxiii–xxiv
    Spratling influenced by, xxiii, 97–99
    Styles influenced by, 138
    Varner and, 40–41
    Walker influenced by, 122
    Woolworth's Lunch Counter protests, xxiii, 104, 105
Clark, Julia, 43, 46–47
Clark Atlanta University (formerly Clark College), 10–11, 59, 138
Clay, Bill, 40, 43
Cleveland Press, 177
Clinton, Bill, 80, 127
CN2 News, 75
CNN, 80, 198
Coastal Virginia Magazine, 80–81
Coleman, Milton, 45, 73, 159
Collegian, The, 2
Colorado Association of Black Journalists, 91, 92
Columbia College, 55
Columbia Journalism Review, 14
Columbia University
    awards and recognition by, 68, 80, 137
    Gilliam at, xxii, 27, 28
    Styles's family and, 138
    Summer Program for Minority Journalists, 3, 60, 89–90
Columbus (GA) Enquirer, 12
Coming Full Circle: From Jim Crow to Journalism (Lloyd), 57, 58, 59, 60, 68
Commercial Appeal, The, 167–170
Communist Workers Party, 107
Community Champion Award, 120
Confederate symbols, dismantling of, 197

Index

Cooke, Janet, 192
Cosby Show, The, 111
Cottman, Michael H., 76
"Countdown to 60" (Spratling), 98–99
Courier-News, 150
COVID-19 pandemic, 26
Cronkite, Walter, 18
Cross, Tiffany D., 198
Cross Connection, The, 198
Crosswalk.com, 178
Cullen, George E., Jr., 51
Curly, John C., *185*
Currie, Phil, 66
Curtis, Mary, 187
Cutler, Jill, 50

Daily Press (Newport News), 7, 49–52, 54, 80
Daily Tar Heel, 106
Daily Texan, 20
Daily Trojan, 3
Daily World, 129
Dallas Fort-Worth Association of Black Journalists Lifetime Achievement Award, 24
Dallas Morning News, 20, 21–22, 24, 142, 198
Dallas Post Tribune, 21
Dateline, 70
Davenport, Janet, 26, 31
Davis, Angela, 33
Dawkins, Wayne, 23
Daye, Charlie Alfred, 163
Days, Michael, 186–187, 188, 189, 192
Deadline, 60
DeLaine, Joseph, 89
Delaney, Paul, 187, 193

Delta Sigma Theta Sorority, Inc., 106, 112
Denver Center Theatre Company, 92
Denver Newspaper Guild Award for Excellence in Journalism for Commentary, 91
Denver Post, 90–91, 92
DeRamus, Betty, 101
Detroit Free Press, xxiii, 97–98, 99, 101–102, 116
Detroit News, 101, 114–116
Detroit riots, xxiv
Dillard, Sandra C., 86–93
   awards and recognition for, 90–91
   career of, 86–93
   education, training, and fellowships of, 88–90, 93
   Maynard Institute and, 89–90, 92
   NABJ and, 86–87, 92, 93
   observations on journalism, 92–93
   personal history of, 86, 87–88, 93
   photograph of, *86*
   racial issues and, 86–93
   sexism experiences of, 87, 91
Dingle, Derek T., 149
Distinguished Consumer Service award, 120
Dixon, Phillip, 192
Dodson, Angela P., 181–189
   awards and recognition for, 184
   career of, 182–189, 192, 193, 194
   education, training, and internships of, 181–182, 183–184, 186
   Lamb influenced by, 192, 193, 194
   NABJ and, 185–186
   observations on journalism, 188–189
   personal history of, 181–182, 183, 186–189

Index

photographs of, *181, 185, 188*
racial issues and, 182–189
Dojcsak, Joseph, 2–3
Douglas, Kirk, 139
Dow Jones Newspaper Fund, 58, 59, 68, 156, 159
Draften, DeWayne, 187
Dry-Burton, Gaile, 76
Dunford, Earle, 34
Dunnigan, Alice Allison, 199–200
Dyson, Michael Eric, 75

Ebony
 Bridges influenced by, 2
 Ciara's "Ebony Power 150 Organization Leader" award, 81
 demise of, 173
 Gilliam's work for, 28
 Norment's work for, 167–174
 Reynolds at, 177
 Ross influenced by, 129
Edge of Change: Women in the Twenty-First Century Press, The (Lloyd, co-editor), 68
Edmonds, Rayful, 44
education. *See also specific institutions*
 Adams's, 175–176, 177
 Adams-Wade's, 17–18, 19–20, 21
 Bridges's, 2–4, 5
 Ciara's, 79, 82–84
 Ciara's work in, 79
 Dillard's, 88–90, 93
 Dillard's work in, 88–89, 92
 Dodson's, 181–182, 183–184, 186
 Farmer's, 33–34, 35
 Farmer's coverage of, 33, 34–35
 Flono's, 10–11, 12, 14, 15
 Flono's coverage of, 14–15

Gaines's, 70, 71–72, 73, 76
Heard's, 156
Henderson's, 112–113, 114, 116
Henderson's work in, 117
Hughes's, 161, 162–163
Hughes's work in, 166
integration vs. segregation of, xxi, 17, 28, 50, 89, 104, 112, 137–138
Israel's, 103–107
Johnson's, 147–148, 149, 151, 153
Johnson's work in, 149, 151, 153
Lamb's, 190–191, 196
Lamb's work in, 195–196
Lloyd's, 58–60, 62, 64–65
Lloyd's work in, 58, 60, 65–66, 68
Maynard Institute for (*see* Maynard Institute for Journalism Education)
Norment's, 169
Ross's, 129–131, 134
Solomon's, 49, 50–51
Solomon's work in, 55
Spratling's, 98, 99–100, 101
Styles's, 138–139, 141
Styles's work in, 140–142
Varner's, 40–41, 42–43, 47
Varner's work in, 41, 45
Walker's, 122
Walker's work in, 120
Education Writers Association, 35
Edward R. Murrow Award, 81, 162
Eisenhower, Dwight, 200
Equal Employment Opportunity Commission, 109
Essence, 71, 195
Eugene O'Neill critic fellowship, 90
European Communities's Visitors Program, 162

Index

Evans, Mari, 141
Exceptional Women in Publishing, 93

Fair Housing Act of 1968, xxiii
Farmer, Robin, 32–35
   awards and recognition for, 33, 35
   Black journalists influencing, 32–33
   career of, 33–35
   education and fellowship of, 33–34, 35
   Maynard Institute and, 34
   personal history of, 33, 35
   photograph of, *32*
   racial issues and, 33–35
Farrakhan, Louis, 6–7
Federal Communications Commission (FCC), 123, 139
FierceforBlackWomen.com, 196
Fitzhugh-Craig, Michelle, 86, 93
Fitzpatrick, Al, 191
Flono, Adam, 10
Flono, Fannie, 9–16
   activism and leadership of, 9–10, 13–15
   awards and recognition for, 15
   career of, 11–16
   curiosity of, 11
   education, training, and internships of, 10–11, 12, 14, 15
   legacy of, 15–16
   NABJ and, 13
   observations on journalism, 15–16
   personal history of, 10
   photograph of, *9*
   racial issues and, 11–12, 13–15
   as riot observer, 9–10, 11
Flono, Prudence, 10
Florida Today, 177
Floyd, George, 24–25, 27, 68, 76, 125, 197, 199
Ford, Harold E., Sr., 169
Foster, Dickie, 21
Fox News, 123
Franklin, Aretha, 99
Fraser, C. Gerald, 187, 193
Frazier, Darnella, 199
Freedom Forum Diversity Institute, 65–66, 68, 176
Frye, Marquette, xxi, 1
Fuller, Catherine, 75

Gaines, Eleanor Murrell, 70
Gaines, Ernest, 184
Gaines, Patrice, 69–77
   awards and recognition for, 76
   Black community advocacy of, 69, 73, 74–76
   career of, 69–77
   education, training, and fellowship of, 70, 71–72, 73, 76
   Maynard Institute and, 71–72
   NABJ and, 76
   observations on journalism, 77
   personal history of, 70–71, 72, 74, 76–77
   photograph of, *69*
   racial issues and, 69–70, 72–77
Gaines, William Baxter, 70
Gannett
   Dodson's work for, 184–185
   Greenville (SC) News ownership, 66

Index

Hughes receiving "Best of Gannett" awards, 162
Johnson hired by, 149–150
Montgomery (AL) Advertiser ownership, 66
Oakland Tribune purchased from, 4
Tennessean ownership, 4
USA Today ownership, 63, 65, 66
GAPP (Greensboro Association of Poor People), 105
Gardner, Mary, 20
Garland Journals, 24
GateHouse Media, 150
gender discrimination. *See* sexism and sexual harassment
Georgia State University, 130, 131
Gilliam, Dorothy Butler, 26–31
   career of, xxii, 27–31, 189
   Dodson's work with, 189
   education, training, and internships of, 27, 28
   legacy of, 29–30
   Maynard Institute and, 29
   NABJ and, 29
   personal history of, 28, 30
   photographs of, *26*, *29*
   pioneering efforts of, xxii, 27–29, 31
   racial and gender issues and, xxii, 26–31
   religion and spirituality of, 28, 30–31
Ginsburg, Ruth Bader, 75
Giovanni, Nikki, 106
Godwin, Kimberly, 197
Golden, Marita, 159
Goldman, Ron, 6
Goode, Wilson, Sr., 34

Graham, Billy, 119, 121, 126
Graham, Donald, 73–74
Graham, Katharine Meyer, 74
Graham, Leroy, 121
Graham, Mary Lee, 121–122
Graham, Phillip L., 74
Grapevine Journal, 100
Gray, Freddie Carlos, Jr., 7–8
Green, Al, 168, 172
Green Book, 184
Greene, Marcia, 63
Greensboro Association of Poor People (GAPP), 105
Greensboro Chamber of Commerce, 162
Greensboro (NC) Daily News, 47, 102, 106, 107–108, 166
Greensboro News & Record, 14, 154
Greensboro Truth and Reconciliation Commission, 108
Greenville (SC) News, 12, 57, 65
Greenville (SC) Piedmont, 12
Gruner & Jahr, 195
"Guilty Until Proven Innocent" project, 81

Haas, R. E. "Buster," 21
Haines, Errin, 198
Hairston, Keith, 76
Haley, Alex, 19, 151
Hall, Tamron, 198
Hampton (VA) Monitor, 50, 51
Hampton Roads Black Media Professionals, 81
Hampton University, 50, 51, 72, 79
Hannah-Jones, Nikole, 198–199
Hardy, Katrice, 198
Harris, Jay, 192
Hartford Courant, 31, 34

Index

Harvard University, 14, 15
Harvey, Steve, 172
Heard, Deborah, 155–160
   career of, 155–160
   education and internships of, 156
   observations on journalism, 159–160
   personal history of, 156–157
   photographs of, *155*, *157*, *159*
   racial and gender issues for, 158–160
Heart & Soul magazine, 178, 195
Henderson, Angelo B., 114, 115–116
Henderson, Angelo Grant, 115
Henderson, Felecia, 111–117
   career of, 111–117
   community advocacy by, 111–112, 114–115, 117
   education and training of, 112–113, 114, 116
   journalists influencing, 113
   Maynard Institute and, 114, 117
   observations on journalism, 117
   personal history of, 112–113, 114, 115–116
   photographs of, *111*, *115*, *117*
   racial issues and, 111–114, 117
Hill, Cathy Gant, 39, 47, 97, 102, 147, 154, 161, 166
"History Makers" project, 81, 174
Hooks, Benjamin, 170
Horner, Cynthia, 33
Housing and Urban Development, Department of, 43, 46
Houston, Whitney, 170, 172
Houston Chronicle, 142, 198
Howard University, 51, 106, 191, 192, 195–196, 199
Howze, Karen, 71

Hudson, Jennifer, 172
Hughes, Allan, 165
Hughes, Larry, 165
Hughes, Larry, Jr., 165
Hughes, Sandra Daye, 161–166
   awards and recognition for, 162, 166
   career of, 161–166
   civil rights movement influencing opportunities for, 162, 163–164
   education of, 161, 162–163
   NABJ and, 162
   personal history of, 163, 165–166
   photograph of, *161*
   racial issues and, 161–166
Hughes, Tiffany, 165
Hunter-Gault, Charlayne, 60
Huntington Advertiser, 182, 184
Hurston, Zora Neal, 141, 159

Ida B. Wells Award for Media Diversity, 68
Ida B. Wells Society for Investigative Reporting, 199
Ifill, Gwen, 39
I Messenger Media, 24
Innocence Project, 75
Inside Politics Sunday, 198
Institute for Educational Inquiry, 14
Institute for Journalism Education, 4
International Civil Rights Center and Museum, 162
Israel, Mae, 103–110
   career of, 103–104, 106–110
   civil rights movement influencing, 104–105
   education, training, and internship of, 103–107

Index

NABJ and, 109
observations on journalism, 110
personal history of, 103–105, 108
photograph of, *103*
racial issues and, 103–110
stutter of, 103, 108
Israel, Mae (mother), 104
Israel, Samuel, 104–105
Ithaca Journal, 147, 148–149, 150, 152, 192

Jackson, Cathy M., 78, 85
Jackson, Janet, 170–171, 172
Jackson, Maynard, Jr., 131
Jackson State University, 176, 177
Jacksonville State University, 156
Jarrett, Vernon, 102
Jennings, Peter, 84
Jet, 28, 129
John H. Johnson Day Award, 174
Johnson, Al, 13, 52
Johnson, John H., 167, 171–174
Johnson, Lynda Bird, 20
Johnson, Lyndon B., xxiv, 3, 20
Johnson, Pam McAllister, 147–154
awards and recognition for, 153
career of, 147–154, 192
education, internships, and fellowships of, 147–148, 149, 151, 153
education positions of, 149, 151, 153
leadership of, 147–154
NABJ and, 153
observations on journalism, 153–154
personal history of, 151–152
photograph of, *147*
racial issues and, 147–154
sexism experiences of, 147–148
Johnson, Robert, 195
Johnson, Sadeqa, 111, 117
Johnson C. Smith University, 15, 71
Johnson Publications, 129
Jones, Georgia, 82, 84
Jones, Jackie, 74–75
Jones, Rashida, 197
Jordan, Carmelie, 191
Journatic News Service, 55
Justice, U.S. Department of, 138

Kagan, Elena, 75
Kansas State University, 151
Kaufman, Monica, 113
Kennedy, John F., xxi, xxiv, 17, 18, 188, 200
Kennedy, Robert F., xxiv
Kennedy, Shawn, 193
Kennedy, Ted, 136
Kerner Commission Report (1968), xxiv–xxv, 3, 143, 164, 177, 184
Kettering Foundation, 14–15
Keys, Alicia, 172
Kincaid, Jim, 80
King, B. B., 51
King, Gayle, 198
King, Martin Luther, Jr.
assassination of, xxiv, 21, 40–41, 72, 151, 197
"I Have a Dream" speech by, xxi, 17–18
Styles influenced by, 138
King, Rodney Glen, 6, 131–132
Knight, Gladys, 111
Knight Fellowship, 40, 46

Index

Knight-Lenfest Table Stakes newsroom innovation program, 117
Knight Ridder, 12, 49
Knowles, Beyoncé, 172
Ku Klux Klan (KKK), 11, 20–21, 107, 137–138
Kuralt, Charles, 140
KYW TV-3, 34
KZAZ-TV, 79, 83–84

Labor Department's Office of Federal Contract Compliance Programs, 134–135
Lamb, Yanick Rice, 190–196
   career of, 190–196
   education of, 190–191, 196
   mentors and journalists influencing, 191, 192–193, 194
   NABJ and, 191
   observations on journalism, 196
   personal history of, 190–191, 194
   photograph of, *190*
   racial issues and, 191–196
   voiceless and community advocacy by, 191–192, 193–195
Land Beyond the River, A (Mitchell), 89
Lantern, 191
Latimer, Leah, 39
Laughing in the Dark: From Colored Girl to Woman of Color—A Journey from Prison to Power (Gaines), 70, 72
Law, Ella P., 58, 68
Lee, Debra, 195
Lee, Robert E. statue of, 197
Lee, Spike, 171
Lee Industries, 35
Lennon, John, 186
Leonard, Bill, 140
"Letters from the Hood" project, 81
Lewis, John, 131
Lincoln Echo, 103
Lincoln University, 28
Lipinski, Anne Marie, 55
Little, Malcolm. *See* Malcolm X
Lloyd, Wanda, 57–68
   awards and recognition for, 68
   career of, 57–68, 176–177
   education, training, and internship of, 58–60, 62, 64–65
   education positions of, 58, 60, 65–66, 68
   Maynard Institute and, 60, 64–65
   mentoring by, 68, 176–177
   NABJ and, 66, 68
   personal history of, 58, 60–61, 64, 65
   photographs of, *57, 67, 68*
   racial issues and, 57–58, 60–61, 63–68
   sexual harassment of, 62
Lloyd, Willie, 61
Local News on Cable (LNC), 79
Long, Earl, 184
Lorillard Tobacco Company, 104
Los Angeles City College, 2
Los Angeles Times, 2
Los Angeles Times / Washington Post News Service, 62–63
Louisville Courier-Journal, 111, 113–114, 171, 186–187

Index

Mackenzie Dial, 100
Macon Telegraph, 11
Madison, Paula, 171
magazines. *See* newspaper and print media; *specific publications*
Malcolm and Me (Farmer), 33
Malcolm X, xxiv, 98
Mandela, Nelson, 99
March on Washington for Jobs and Freedom, xxi, 17, 40
Marquette University, 34
Marshall University, 181–182, 184
Martin, Ron, 64
Martin, Trayvon, 45–46
Matabane, Paula, 196
Matthews, Chris, 198
Matthews, Lamar, 130
Maya Angelou and Friends seminar series, 141
Maya Angelou Women Who Lead Award, 15
Maynard, Nancy Hicks, 3–4, 23
Maynard, Robert "Bob," 3–4, 23, 60, 72, 89–90, 193
Maynard Institute for Journalism Education
    Adams-Wade and, 23–24
    Bridges and, 4, 5, 7
    Dillard and, 89–90, 92
    Farmer and, 34
    Gaines and, 71–72
    Gilliam and, 29
    Henderson and, 114, 117
    Lloyd and, 60, 64–65
    Summer Program for Minority Journalists, 3–4, 23–24, 34, 60, 71–72, 89–90
    transition to, 4
McAllister, Elmer, 152
McAllister, Esther, 152
McCall, Nathan, 149
McElvene, Clyde, 159
McLaine, Shirley, 90
media. *See* news media
Media General Inc., 34
Meeting at the Table: African-American Women Write on Race, Culture and Community (Lloyd and McElroy), 68
Memphis State University, 169
Mens et Manus: A Pictorial History of North Carolina Agricultural & Technical State University (Styles), 142
mentorships
    Adams's, 176–177, 179–180
    Ciara's, 83
    Gilliam's, 28, 30
    Heard's, 159
    industry promotion of, 159, 177, 199
    Johnson's, 149, 153
    Lamb's, 191, 192
    Lloyd's, 68, 176–177
    NABJ championing, 177
    Norment's, 169
    Ross's, 135
    Spratling's, 101
    Varner's, 43
    Walker's, 120
Metro Seven, 63–64, 109–110
Meyer, Eugene, 74
Miami Herald, 57, 61, 142, 156–157, 158, 198
Miami News, 72
Michigan Press Association, 101
Michigan State University, 100, 102
Miller, Ron, 123

Million Man March, 6–7
Minikus, Lee W., xxi, 1
Mitchell, John, Jr., 197
Mitchell, Loften, 89
Mitchum, Robert, 139
Miyan Communications Group, 196
Moments of Grace: Meeting the Challenge to Change (Gaines), 76
Montel Williams Show, The, 178
Montgomery (AL) Advertiser, 57, 66–68
Montgomery Bus Boycott, xxiii, 67, 97–98
Montiel, Steve, 5
Moore, Acel, 186
Moore, Pam, 113
Morehouse College, 142
Morgan, Diana, 79
Morgan, Thomas, 187
Morgan State University, 75
Motown, xxiii
MSNBC, 142, 158, 197–198
Murray State News, 113
Murray State University, 112, 113

NAACP, 12, 102, 105, 132, 170
NABJ. *See* National Association of Black Journalists
NABJ Journal, 64
National Academy of Television Arts and Sciences Gold and Silver Circle, 121
National Advisory Commission on Civil Disorders, xxiv, 177. *See also Kerner Commission Report* (1968)
National Association of Black Journalists (NABJ)
    Adams-Wade in, 22–23, 24
    Chuck Stone Lifetime Achievement Award, 162
    Ciara's leadership of, 81
    Dillard and, 86–87, 92, 93
    Dodson and, 185–186
    Flono in, 13
    formation of, 22–23, 86–87, 102, 186
    Gaines and, 76
    Gilliam in, 29
    Hall of Fame of, 68, 153, 174
    Hughes honored by, 162
    Israel and, 109
    Johnson and, 153
    Lamb and, 191
    Lloyd and, 66, 68
    mentorships championed by, 177
    Norment and, 171, 174
    Salute to Excellence Award, 99, 101
    Solomon in, 53
    Spratling and, 99, 101, 102
National Association of Minority Media Executives, 66, 68
National Geographic, 102
National Guard, xxi, xxii, 1, 6, 17, 105
National Museum of African American History and Culture, 176
National Public Radio (NPR), 9, 75, 79, 80
National Theater Critics conference, 92
Naylor, Gloria, 73
NBC, 198
NBC-12 Richmond, 118, 120, 121, 123–126

Index

"Negro Motorist Green Book, The," 184
Neighbors NW, 157
Neuharth, Allen, 150
New Journal and Guide, 135
Newsday, 49, 51–52, 193
Newseum, *159*, 176
News-Journal, 3
news media. *See also* broadcast media; newspaper and print media; *specific news organizations and journalists*
    civil rights movement coverage by, xxiii–xxiv
    current diversity and inclusion in, 197–198
    Kerner Commission Report influence on, xxiv–xxv, 3, 143, 164, 177, 184
    Million Man March coverage by, 6–7
    riot coverage by, xxii, 2, 11
    shield laws for, 72
newspaper and print media. *See also specific news organizations*
    Adams's work in, 176–180
    Adams-Wade's work in, 19–25
    Bridges's work in, 2–8
    Ciara's work in, 80
    current diversity and inclusion in, 198
    Dillard's work in, 87, 89–93
    Dodson's work in, 182–189, 192, 193, 194
    Farmer's work in, 33–35
    Flono's work in, 9–16
    Gaines's work in, 69–77
    Gilliam's work in, xxii, 27–31
    Heard's work in, 155–160
    Henderson's work in, 111, 113–117
    Israel's work in, 103–104, 106–110
    Johnson's work in, 147–154, 192
    Kerner Commission Report influence on, xxv, 164, 177, 184
    Lamb's work in, 190–196
    layoffs and downsizing in, 7, 35, 55, 66–67, 133, 142, 178, 198
    Lloyd's work in, 57–68, 176–177
    Norment's work in, 167–174
    Ross's work in, 127–135
    shield laws for, 72
    Solomon's work in, 49–56
    Spratling's work in, xxiii, 97–102
    Varner's work in, 39–41, 42, 44–47
New York Association of Black Journalists (NYABJ), 194
New York Times
    Caldwell at, 72
    Ciara's work for, 80
    current diversity and inclusion in, 198–199
    Dodson at, 183, 187–189, 193, 194
    Hannah-Jones at, 198–199
    Lamb at, 192, 193–195
    lawsuits against, 187
    Maynard at, 4
New York Times Magazine, 198
New York University, 138
Nieman Fellowship, 4, 14, 15
19th, The, 198
Nixon, Richard and administration, 61–62, 72

Index

Norfolk State University, 85, 149
Norma Adams-Wade NABJ Founders Scholarship, 24
Norment, Lynn, 167–174
   awards and recognition for, 170, 174
   career of, 167–174
   celebrity interviews by, 168, 170–172
   education and internship of, 169
   NABJ and, 171, 174
   observations on journalism, 174
   personal history of, 167, 168–169, 171
   photographs of, *167, 170, 173*
   racial issues and, 167–174
   sexism experiences of, 170–171
Norris, Michele, 39
North Carolina Agricultural and Technical (A&T) State University, 104, 105, 141–142, 161, 162–163, 166
North Carolina Society of Historians, 142
Northshield, Robert, 140
North Texas Legends Awards, 24
Northwestern University, 64, 138–139
NPR (National Public Radio), 9, 75, 79, 80
NYABJ (New York Association of Black Journalists), 194

Oakland Tribune, 4, 23, 193
Oatman, Charles, 9–10
Obama, Barack, 14, 55, 80, *80*, 133, 172, 189
Obama, Michelle, 172

Obama's Legacy: What He Accomplished as President (Days), 189
Ohio State University, 191
On Detroit, 114–115
Onyx, 191
Oprah, 99, 175, 178
Order of the Long Leaf Pine, 162
Our Choking Times, 191

Paley, William B., 140
Parks, Rosa, xxiii, 97–98
Parthenon, 182
pay disparities, 49, 53, 73–74
Payne, Ethel, 199
Peabody Award, 136
People's Choice, 100
Perry, DeVeen, 112
Perry, Harmon, 129
Perry, Maxine, 99–100
Philadelphia Daily News, 22, 32
Philadelphia Inquirer, 186, 188
Phillip, Abby, 198
Pima Community College, 83
Pine Bluff Commercial, 176
Pittsburgh Courier, 183
Pittsburgh Post Gazette, 183
PM Magazine, 162
police behavior
   Adams's experiences with, 176
   Dillard's reporting on, 91–92
   George Floyd death and, 24–25, 27, 68, 76, 125, 197, 199
   Freddie Gray death and, 7–8
   Kerner Commission Report on, xxiv
   Rodney King and, 6, 131–132
   Lloyd's leadership and, 65
   riots, protests, and, xxi–xxii, 1, 6, 9–10, 24–25, 26, 105, 107, 131–132

Index

Stone reporting on, 32
Styles's experiences with, 138
Walker's experiences with, 119, 124–126
Press Club of Dallas' Excellence in Journalism, 24
Primetime Live, 114
Prince, 170
print media. *See* newspaper and print media
protests. *See* riots and protests
Providence Bulletin, 60
Providence (RI) Evening Bulletin, 57, 60–61
Providence Journal, 51
Pulitzer Prizes
    Cooke's, 192
    Denver Post's, 90, 91
    Dillard's team, 91
    Frazier's citation at, 199
    Hannah-Jones's, 198
    A. Henderson's, 115
    Oakland Tribune's, 40
    Varner's nomination for, 40, 45
    Wilkerson's, 194
    Williams's, 35
    Wilson's, 89
Pulley, Brett, 187
Purdue/Indiana University, 141

Queen Latifah, 172

racial issues. *See also* segregation
    Adams and, 176–177, 180
    Adams-Wade and, 20–22, 24–25
    affirmative action and, 40, 45, 106, 123, 134, 139–140, 147
    AP complaints and lawsuit over, 134–135
    Ciara and, 79–81, 84
    civil rights movement on (*see* civil rights movement)
    continuing injustice and, xxv, 143, 197, 199–200
    current improvements to, 197–199
    Dillard and, 86–93
    Dodson and, 182–189
    Farmer and, 33–35
    Flono and, 11–12, 13–15
    Gaines and, 69–70, 72–77
    Gilliam and, xxii, 26–31
    Heard and, 158–160
    Henderson and, 111–114, 117
    Hughes and, 161–166
    Israel and, 103–110
    Johnson and, 147–154
    Kerner Commission Report on, xxiv–xxv, 3, 143, 164, 177, 184
    Lamb and, 191–196
    Lloyd and, 57–58, 60–61, 63–68
    NABJ addressing (*see* NABJ)
    Norment and, 167–174
    pay disparities as, 49, 53, 73–74
    riots and protests over (*see* riots and protests)
    Ross and, 129–135
    Solomon and, 49–55
    Spratling and, xxiii, 97–102
    Styles and, 137–143
    Varner and, 40–43, 45–46
    Walker and, 120–126
    Washington Post sued over, 63–64, 109–110
radio. *See* broadcast media

Radio and Television News Directors Association, 81
Rashad, Phylicia, 111
Rather, Dan, 80
Rattley, Jessie, 50
Read Charlotte, 15
Reed, Julia Scott, 19, 21
Reeve, Maria, 198
Reid, Daphne Maxwell, 179
Reid, Joy, 197–198
Reid, Russell E., 48–49
Reid Out, The, 198
religion and spirituality
  Adams's, 175, 178, 179
  Adams-Wade's, 19
  in Dallas Black community, 22
  Farmer and, 33
  Gaines's, 77
  Gilliam's, 28, 30–31
  Green's focus on, 168
  Henderson's, 116
  Hughes's, 165
  Ross's, 128, 135
  Walker's, 122, 126
Remember the Ladies (Dodson), 189
Republican, 31
Reuters, 137
Reynolds, Barbara, 176–177
Rhoden, William "Bill," 193
Rice, William, 191
Richardson, Monica, 198
Richmond Magazine, 33
Richmond News Leader, 35
Richmond Planet, The, 197
Richmond Times-Dispatch, 34–35, 51, 135, 178–180, 198
Richmond Times-Dispatch-Dow Jones Urban Journalism Workshop, 179–180

Right On, 33
riots and protests
  Augusta, 9–10, 11
  Birmingham, 18
  Black Lives Matter, 27, 30–31
  Chicago, 151
  Ciara's role in, 82–83
  civil rights (*see* civil rights movement)
  Detroit, xxiv
  George Floyd death leading to, 24–25, 27, 197
  Greensboro, 107–108
  Israel influenced by, 105, 107–108
  Kerner Commission Report on, xxiv, 3, 143, 164, 177, 184
  Los Angeles/Rodney King, 6, 131–132
  Miami, 72
  Omaha, 91
  Watts, xxi–xxii, 1–2
Rivet360, 55
Robert C. Maynard Institute for Journalism Education. *See* Maynard Institute for Journalism Education
Robert G. McGruder Award for Media Diversity, 68
Robertson, Denise. *See* Bridges, Denise
Robinson, Ernest L., 50
Robinson, Eugene, 158
Robinson, Fannie Celeste Gillis, 50
Robinson, Max, 193
Rochester Times Union, 186
Roots (Haley), 19, 151
Ross, Sonya, 127–135
  Black community coverage by, 129, 131–132, 135

Index

career of, 127–135
education, training, and internship of, 129–131, 134
observations on journalism, 135
personal history of, 129–130, 133
photograph of, *127*
racial issues and, 129–135
source cultivation by, 131
in White House Press Corps, 127–129, 132–133
Ryan, April, 200

Sales, Soupy, 184
Sandra and Friends, 162, 164–165
Saturday Evening Post, 2
Savannah Evening Press, 59
Savannah State College (now Savannah State University), 58, 59, 68, 140–141
Say Their Names: How Black Lives Came to Matter in America (Gaines, contributor), 76
Schneider, Joan, 139
School Bell Award, 101
Scott, Warren, 93
Scripps National Spelling Bee, 87–88
Seattle Post-Intelligencer, 40, 45
Seattle Times, 40, 45–46
segregation
  bus rider, xxiii, 67, 97–98
  Dallas's de facto, 22
  educational, xxi, 17, 28, 50, 89, 104, 112, 137–138
  Gilliam's pioneering despite, 27–28
  Israel's experiences with, 104, 105–106
  Lloyd's experiences with, 57, 58
  Spratling's experiences with, 100
  Styles's experiences with, 137–139
  Varner's experiences with, 41
September 11, 2001 terrorist attacks, 128–129
Serrell, Doris Crawford Adams, 19
sexism and sexual harassment
  Ciara's experiences with, 82–83
  coeducation lawsuit vs., 122
  Dillard's experiences with, 87, 91
  Gaines's experiences with, 70
  Gilliam's experiences with, xxii, 27–28
  Hannah-Jones's experiences with, 199
  Hughes's experiences with, 164
  Johnson's experiences with, 147–148
  Lloyd's experiences with, 62
  Norment's experiences with, 170–171
  pay disparities and, 73–74
  Washington Post sued over, 110
Shahid, Sharon, 176–177
shield laws, 72
Shipp, E. R., 193
Siloam School, 15
Simmons, Bernadine "Bernie," 121
Simpson, Nicole Brown, 6
Simpson, O. J., 6, 7
1619 Project, 198
60 Minutes, 80, 137, 140
Smalls, John Henry, 58
Smalls, Wanda. *See* Lloyd, Wanda
Smith, Tammie, 127, 135
Smith, Will, 172
Solomon, Linwood, 52–54
Solomon, Sheila Robinson, 48–56
  career of, 49–56

Index

education, training, and internships of, 49, 50–51
NABJ and, 53
Obama and, 55
observations on journalism, 55, 56
patience, perseverance, and unselfishness of, 49, 51, 55
personal history of, 48–49, 50, 52–54
photographs of, *48, 52*
racial issues and, 49–55
Soros Justice Media Fellowship, 76
South Bend Tribune, 100–101
Speak to My Heart (Adams), 178
Spelman College, 58, 59, 60, 68, 76, 138–139
Spelman Spotlight, 59
Spirit of Diversity Award, 102
spirituality. *See* religion and spirituality
Spratling, Annie Lou, 99
Spratling, Cassandra, 97–102
   awards and recognition for, 99, 101–102
   Black community advocacy by, 97–102
   Black journalists influencing, 101, 102
   career of, xxiii, 97–102
   civil rights movement influence on, xxiii, 97–99
   education, training, and internship of, 98, 99–100, 101
   NABJ and, 99, 101, 102
   observations on journalism, 102
   personal history of, 98, 99
   photograph of, *97*
   racial issues and, xxiii, 97–102
Spratling, Fletcher, 99
Stanford University, 40
Starr, Blaze, 184
Stevenson, Adlai, II, 24
Stone, Chuck, 22, 32–33, 162
Stories That Cover Us: Meditations and Fiber Art by the Pacific Northwest African American Quilters (Varner, co-author), 40
St. Paul Pioneer Press, 156
Styles, Gwenelle, 138
Styles, Jennie, 138
Styles, Julian (father), 138
Styles, Julian (son), 138
Styles, Marty, 138
Styles, Teresa J., 136–143
   awards and recognition for, 136–137, 142
   career of, 136–143
   civil rights movement influencing, 138
   education of, 138–139, 141
   education positions of, 140–142
   legacy of, 137
   observations on journalism, 142–143
   personal history of, 138–139
   photograph of, *136*
   racial issues and, 137–143
Summer Institute in Black Repertory Theatre, 89
Summer Program for Minority Journalists, 3–4, 23–24, 34, 60, 71–72, 89–90
Swenson, Paul, 58

Index

Teddy, 143
Teen Times, 59
television. *See* broadcast media
Temple University, 59–60
Tennessean, 5–7, 135
Texas Instruments, 21
Texas Metro News, 24
Their Eyes Were Watching God (Hurston), 141
theroot.com, 33
This Week in Hampton Roads, 79
Thomas, Cal, 7
Thomas, Helen, 39, 44
Thomas, Wendy, 7
Thriving in the Shadows: The Black Experience in Charlotte and Mecklenburg County (Flono), 15
Time magazine, 51–52, 60
tokenism, xxv
Toledo Blade, 192
Tom Joyner Morning Show, 80
"Tough Boys and Trouble— Those Girls Waiting Outside D.C. Jail Remind Me of Myself" (Gaines), 76
"Trading Places: From the Newsroom to the Classroom" (Farmer), 35
Trailblazer: A Pioneering Journalist's Fight to Make the Media Look More Like America (Gilliam), 27, 189
Trescott, Jacqueline, 71–72
Tribune Company, 49, 54–55
Tri-State Defender, 28
Truman, Harry, 199
Trump, Donald, 200
Tucker, C. Delores, 132

Turner, Henry McNeal, 139
Turner, Ike, 171
Turner, Ted, 139
Turner, Tina, 171–172
27 Views of Charlotte: The Queen City in Prose and Poetry (Flono, contributor), 15
Tyson, Cicely, 184

UNC-TV, 141
United Press International (UPI), 39, 40, 44, 81, 137
Unity of Journalists of Color, 29
University of Alabama, xxi, 17, 156
University of Arizona, 82–83, 114
University of California, Berkeley, 3, 34, 71, 92. *See also* Maynard Institute for Journalism Education
University of California, Santa Barbara, 89
University of Denver, 88, 90
University of the District of Columbia, 73
University of Georgia, Athens, 129–130
University of Maryland, 43
University of Memphis journalism awards, 174
University of Michigan, 35, 101
University of Mississippi, 28
University of Missouri, 156
University of New Mexico, 5
University of North Carolina, Chapel Hill, 106–107, 138, 141–142, 198–199
University of North Carolina, Greensboro, 104

Index

University of North Carolina Board of Governors Awards for Teaching Excellence, 142
University of South Carolina, 12
University of Southern California, 3
University of Texas-Austin, xxi, 17, 18, 20, 21
University of Virginia, 122
University of Wisconsin, Madison, 147–148
UPI (United Press International), 39, 40, 44, 81, 137
USA Today, 57, 63, 64–65, 71, 150, 176

Vanderbilt University, 65. *See also* Freedom Forum Diversity Institute
Vanguarde Media, 195
Varner, Henry, 42, 46–47
Varner, Lynne K., 39–47
    awards and recognition for, 40, 45
    career of, 39–47
    civil rights movement and, 40–41
    education, training, and fellowship of, 40–41, 42–43, 47
    journalists influencing, 39–40, 44
    leadership of, 41–42, 47
    optimism of, 47
    personal history of, 40–41, 42–43, 46–47
    photograph of, *39*
    racial issues and, 40–43, 45–46
Vernon Sparks, Lisa, 198
Virginia Citizens Consumer Council, 120

Virginia Commonwealth University Health Hume-Lee Transplant Center, 120–121
Virginia Communications Hall of Fame, 81, 120
Virginian-Pilot, 7, 79
Virginia Press Association, 7
Virginia State University, 138
Virginia Union University, 122–123
Visit Detroit, 102
Von Drehle, David, 158
Voting Rights Act of 1965, xxiii, 40, 163
Voting Rights March (2015), 99

Wake Forest University, 141
Walker, Diane Graham, 118–126
    awards and recognition for, 120–121
    Black journalists influencing, 121–122
    career of, 118–126
    consumer and community advocacy by, 118–121, 123–126
    education of, 122
    personal history of, 119–120, 121–122, 126
    photographs of, *118, 120, 125*
    police interactions, 119, 124–126
    racial issues and, 120–126
Walker, Gloria, 58
Walker, Oper Lee, 58
Wallace, George C., xxi, 17
Wall Street Journal, 115
Washington, Denzel, 172
Washington, Harold, 170

Index

Washington Post
    Ciara's work for, 80
    Cooke at, 192
    current diversity and inclusion in, 198
    Farmer's work for, 33
    Gaines at, 69, 70–71, 73–76
    Gilliam at, xxii, 27, 28–30, 63
    Heard at, 155–159
    Israel at, 109–110
    Lloyd at, 57, 61–64
    Maynard at, 3–4
    McCall at, 149
    pay disparities at, 73–74
    racial discrimination lawsuit against, 63–64, 109–110
    sexism lawsuit against, 110
    strike at, 62
    Trescott at, 71–72
    Varner at, 39–40, 44–45
    Watergate scandal coverage, 61–62
Washington Star, 72–73, 186
Washington State University, 41
Watergate scandal, 61–62
Watson, Lauren, 91
Watson, Susan, 101
Watts riots, xxi–xxii, 1–2
WAVY-TV, 79
Wayne State University Journalism Institute for Media Diversity, 102
WBBM, 139
WEAA-FM, 75
Wells-Barnett, Ida B., 199
Western Electric, 163
Western Kentucky University, 151, 153
Westworld Productions, 151
WETV (now PBA Atlanta), 139
WFMY, 161–166
WHAS-TV, 113
What Shall We Do About Mother, 143
White, Jack, 60
White House Press Corps, 39, 44, 92, 127–129, 132–133, 199–200
Whitman, Charles, 20
WHRO-TV, 79
Wilkerson, Isabel, 193, 194
Williams, Brittany, 178
Williams, Catherine Walker, 58
Williams, Lena, 187, 193
Williams, Michael Paul, 35
Willie Parker Peace History Book Award, 142
Wilson, August, 89
Wilson, L. Allen, 28
Winston-Salem Journal, 14
Wisconsin Public Broadcasting, 148
WLOU-AM, 114
Wolfe, Shelia, 55
Wolfman, Jon, 132
Wonder, Stevie, 51
Woodson, Mary, 168
Woolworth's Lunch Counter protests, xxiii, 104, 105
WTKR-TV, 79
Wussler, Robert J., 139
WVEC-TV, 79–80

Yale University, 90

Zora Neale Hurston–Richard Wright Foundation, 159

About the Author

Bonnie Newman Davis has been a journalist for more than four decades. But long before she understood the meaning of journalism, Davis, at age three or four, was writing stories "out loud" by recounting the exploits of her maternal grandparents' 10 children - five boys, five girls.

Then in their teens and early twenties, her aunts and uncles lived in a rural part of North Carolina where tobacco reigned. When not attending school or picking tobacco, the Chavis siblings enjoyed the same pastimes as did most young people their age—dressing up for proms or social outings, listening to soulful music on the radio, and driving or riding in fast cars.

That was in the early 1960s. Davis' childhood recitations regarding her large, extended family that she visited each summer offered few hints about the civil and social unrest then swirling across America. Indeed, the famous sit-ins at a Woolworth's lunch counter was within walking distance of her home in Greensboro, North Carolina. Yet, aside from whispers of "curfews" or muffled voices from television newscasters, little about the sit-ins was discussed in Davis' home.

Years later, while in college at North Carolina A&T State University, Davis became more fully aware of the civil rights movement and how,

About the Author

based on the findings of a 1968 Kerner Commission report, much of it tied in with the assassinations of the Rev. Dr. Martin Luther King, Jr. and Robert F. Kennedy years earlier when Davis was in sixth grade.

It also was at A&T that Davis, an English major, wrote her first article after taking a journalism course during her junior year. Her professor published the article in the student newspaper, *The A&T Register*, and it later was picked up by the local Black newspaper, *The Carolina Peacemaker*. Other articles followed, along with a summer internship at the *Wilmington Star News in Wilmington, N.C.*

When Davis graduated from A&T in 1979 with a bachelor's degree in English, she not only understood journalism's meaning and power, she was eager to learn more. A Dow Jones Newspaper Fund internship that summer in Louisville, Kentucky was followed by graduate school at the University of Michigan-Ann Arbor, where she earned a master's degree in journalism in 1980.

After graduate school, Davis became a reporter and editor for the Richmond News Leader and, later, the Richmond Times-Dispatch in Richmond, Virginia. Her areas of coverage included education, government, urban affairs, business, and arts and culture. She also has worked for newspapers in Kentucky, North Carolina, and Michigan, as well as for MSNBC's *thegrio.com* and *BlackAmericaWeb.com*.

Additionally, Davis has served as a journalism professor at Virginia Commonwealth University, the University of North Carolina at Chapel Hill, and North Carolina A&T State University. At NCA&T, Davis held the *Greensboro News & Record-Janice Bryant Howroyd Endowed Professorship*. Other academic appointments have included Hampton, Norfolk State, St. Augustine's, Virginia Union, and Washington and Lee universities.

In 2011, Davis was named Educator of the Year by the National Association of Black Journalists, and she has received several awards and recognition for her work, including a 2007 NABJ Ethel Payne Fellowship to report in Ghana, West Africa.

In 2016, Davis founded the BND Institute of Media and Culture, Inc., a nonprofit organization that presents programs and events focused on African American culture and news media. Her institute also sponsors a summer media camp for middle and high school students.

In May 2022, Davis became managing editor of the *Richmond Free Press,* a 30-year-old Black-owned newspaper in Richmond, Virginia.

In October 2022, Davis was inducted into the Department of Journalism and Mass Communication Hall of Fame at North Carolina Agricultural and Technical State University. The award "honors the pioneers who helped pave the way in Journalism at North Carolina A&T and beyond."

Throughout her career, Davis has been an active leader, member and participant in several civic, social and professional organizations. As a longtime member of the National Association of Black Journalists, she twice formed chapters of the Richmond (Va.) Association of Black Journalists, and served as a regional director and board member for the NABJ. Additionally, Davis has served in local and national leadership positions for the Society of Professional Journalists. Her current civic and social memberships include the Richmond Alumnae Chapter of Delta Sigma Theta Sorority, Inc. and the Original Circle of Friends, a philanthropic organization that raises money for college students.

Davis was married to the late William Haynes Davis and the late Lawrence Eric Stanley. She has one adult daughter, Erin Danielle Stanley, a proud graduate of Spelman College and the University of Chicago's Crown Family School of Social Work, Policy, and Practice.

More about Bonnie Newman Davis

Virginia Press Association
Sept. 28, 2022
https://www.vpa.net/articles/3117/

International Journalists' Network
March 2022
https://ijnet.org/en/story/legacy-black-women-journalists-us

Richmond.com
February 12, 2022
https://richmond.com/opinion/editorial/editorial-black-women-journalists-create-a-lasting-legacy/article_3237c891-787c-5a9f-acd3-69c6d84de504.html

More about Black Women and Women in Journalism

News Leaders Association
https://www.newsleaders.org/2019-diversity-survey-results

USA Today
https://www.usatoday.com/story/opinion/2021/09/01/usa-today-newsroom-now-majority-female-sees-gains-staff-diversity/5659410001/

Women in Journalism
https://www.womeninjournalism.org/hirewomenjourno-all/black-women-journalists-to-follow

Womens Media Center
https://womensmediacenter.com/assets/site/reports/10c550d19ef9f3688f_mlbres2jd.pdf

NPR
https://www.npr.org/sections/thetwo-way/2018/03/07/591513558/women-of-color-are-severely-underrepresented-in-newsrooms-study-says

Yale Daily News
https://yaledailynews.com/sjp/2021/08/28/where-are-the-black-women-journalists-on-television/

Forbes
https://www.forbes.com/sites/jessicagold/2021/10/31/we-need-to-talk-about-the-experiences-of-black-journalists/?sh=1560b19844ff

www.ingramcontent.com/pod-product-compliance
Lightning Source LLC
Chambersburg PA
CBHW031241290426
44109CB00012B/385